The Radical Insufficiency of Human Life

The Radical Insufficiency of Human Life

The Poetry of R. de Castro and J. A. Silva

by AILEEN DEVER

McFarland & Company, Inc., Publishers
Jefferson, North Carolina, and London

Quotations from original Spanish and Galician texts were translated for this work by María del Carmen Dever Luengo and Aileen Dever.

Library of Congress Cataloguing-in-Publication Data

Dever, Aileen.
The radical insufficiency of human life : the poetry of R. de Castro and J. A. Silva / by Aileen Dever.
p. cm.
Includes bibliographical references and index.
ISBN 0-7864-0806-5 (softcover : 55# alkaline paper) ∞
1. Castro, Rosalía de, 1837–1885—Criticism and interpretation. 2. Silva, José Asunción, 1865–1896—Criticism and interpretation. 3. Human beings in literature. I. Title.

PQ6512.C226 Z5484 2000
861'.5—dc21 00-56836

British Library cataloguing data are available

Cover image ©2000 Eyewire

©2000 Aileen Dever. All rights reserved

No part of this book may be reproduced or transmitted in any form or by any means, electronic or mechanical, including photocopying or recording, or by any information storage and retrieval system, without permission in writing from the publisher.

Manufactured in the United States of America

McFarland & Company, Inc., Publishers
Box 611, Jefferson, North Carolina 28640
www.mcfarlandpub.com

INTRODUCTION

¿Por qué nacemos, madre, dime, por qué morimos?
(Why are we born, mother, tell me, why do we die?)
—J. A. Silva, *Gotas amargas* 75 (*Bitter Drops*)

¿Qué somos? ¿Qué es la muerte?
(What are we? What is death?)
—R. de Castro, *Sar* 464

Ortega y Gasset held that a bull always has enough to be a bull but that a human being always lacks what is necessary to be human (1961: 43). This work analyzes the writings of the Spaniard Rosalía de Castro (1837–1885) and the Colombian José Asunción Silva (1865–1896) through a comparative approach never attempted between them and based on the premise that both experience being human as radical insufficiency.[1] Castro and Silva perceive living as defined by deep, unfulfillable needs for direction, purpose, and certainty, a perception that stems largely from their loss of religious beliefs. Readers are drawn to their writings because both authors give eloquent expression to questions and intimate fears about human existence. Both authors filtered their end-of-the-century pessimism through the poetry of Poe, Heine, Bécquer, Hugo, and Campoamor, as well as through the philosophy of Schopenhauer (Camacho Guizado, 1990a: 543; Fogelquist 282; Kulp 13, 15–16, 19, 113; Miramón 66; Tirrell 327). Therefore striking similarities in theme, tone, and style exist between Castro and Silva, each so associated with the native soil (Galicia, Spain/Bogotá, Colombia) that the many points of contact between the two have escaped notice. Yet comparing them also brings to the fore meaningful differences, helping to delineate more precisely the individuality of each writer.

Although they attempted serious prose writing, these authors are remembered essentially as poets because it is through their poetry that they express most purely and sensitively their worldview and personal concerns. It does not seem that either was aware of the other's existence, yet in many ways they are soul mates.[2] Displaying two of the most sincere and suggestive voices of the nineteenth century, they found few readers to understand or appreciate them during their lifetimes. The two authors suffered financial problems and confronted the premature deaths of loved ones, which significantly darkened their worldview.[3] Both possessed melancholy dispositions and composed poetry at an early age. They also shared similar aesthetic inclinations in their affinity and talent for painting.

These writers revealed early their crises of religious faith. Already Castro's spiritual struggle comes to the fore in some of the anguished poems of *La flor* (*The Flower*), written when she was twenty.[4] Silva's poem "Crisálidas" (*Libro de versos* 10, "Cocoons," in *Book of Verses*), published when he was twenty-one, on his sister Inés's death, also indicates metaphysical doubts about the fate of the human soul. Both authors' concern about mortality results in an acute awareness of the passage of time. They also tend to depict human existence as a union of opposites: youth and old age, dreams and crude reality. This perception stems from their idyllic conception of life in childhood, contrasted with disenchanting experiences and realizations in adulthood. Neither wrote plays, but they frequently utilize dialogue in their poems, novels, and short prose pieces to reveal their fundamentally dramatic vision of the world. The prevailing mood in their works is introspective and sad. A common atmosphere pervades: gray mist, cemeteries, and twilight settings. These authors correspond closely in theme: disillusionment with love, loss of faith, and obsession with death.

To lend precision to the comparison, I apply to their writings an original synthesis of three interrelated twentieth-century Spanish thinkers who systematize the intuition of life as radical insufficiency: José Ortega y Gasset, Xavier Zubiri, and Pedro Laín Entralgo. The conception of human life as radical insufficiency stems from Ortega's *Historia como sistema*, 1947 (History as a System), Zubiri's *Sobre el hombre*, 1986 (About Man), and *Estructura dinámica de la realidad*, 1995 (Dynamic Structure of Reality), and Laín's *Antropología médica para clínicos*, 1986 (Medical Anthropology for Clinicians) and *Teatro del mundo*, 1986 (Theatre of the World). The ability of these philosophers to interpret such a perception with precision may stem from their own experience, different from that of the late nineteenth century, when Castro and Silva lived. In these writers' time religious beliefs began to fluctuate; a feeling of crisis was dawning as something new and fearful. However, when Ortega, Zubiri, and Laín wrote, the crisis was no longer a novelty but endemic, habitual, and associated with living, hence, easier to master theoretically. This different experience of crisis as a historical habit arrived around World War II and its immediate aftermath (Laín *Teatro* 327). The thinking of Ortega, Zubiri, and Laín provides precise yet flexible notions that delicately fit the intuitions of living visible in Castro and Silva and clarify them without doing them conceptual violence.

For Ortega, Zubiri, and Laín, being human consists of perceiving life as a series of fundamental lacks. Humans lack a fixed "nature" and have an unfulfillable need to create their own being, which leads to anxiety (Zubiri, 1986: 619–620) and an incorrigible feeling of emptiness (Laín *Antropología* 151–153; Ortega, 1947: 13, 32–33). Unlike a stone, which has an unchanging nature, and unlike a star, which has a set path to follow, humans are unstable beings, needing continually to improvise in a world of uncertainty (Ortega, 1947: 13–14, 33, 40; Zubiri, 1986: 620). Not compelled to act in one way or another, they must decide for themselves how to live meaningful lives (Ortega, 1947: 32–33). Yet as individuals they are plastic entities, constantly refashioning their personalities and outlooks, depending on individual choices and experiences (Ortega, 1947: 34, 36–37, 41–42; Zubiri, 1995: 249–250). It follows that over time human beings change considerably, for better or for worse. Though previously guided by systems of beliefs in religion or in discursive reason, they now must continually improvise orienting principles in a world of uncertainty and crisis (Laín *Antropología* 155; Ortega, 1947: 13–14, 33, 40; Zubiri, 1986: 620). In this regard humans are indigent beings, defined by their needs and wants as they attempt to determine how they should create meaning in their lives (Ortega, 1947: 33).

In their endeavors to be agents, authors, and actors of their own lives, human beings have the potential to become many things. They do not, however, have an infinite number of possibilities because they are limited by their own circumstances, the past, both personal and collective, as well as by the constraints and prejudices of the society and age into which they are born (Zubiri, 1995: 262–263). Appropriately, Ortega calls the human being "un Dios de ocasión" (a God of the occasion) in view of self-creation within the limitation of opportunity (1947: 35). The quest for self-creation increases in difficulty under the pressure of anxiety resulting from the uncertainty inherent in human life. Human beings' beliefs, hopes, and loves are all permeated by uncertainty (Laín *Antropología* 152–153). Humans must continually make choices in their personal and professional lives, but they can never be completely certain that the choices they make are truly the best ones for them. Therefore they live their lives with the anxiety of making errors in judgment. Yet if they could know with certainty which courses were best, they still could not be sure of success in their endeavors because personal shortcomings, bad luck, or circumstances beyond their control can lead to failure (Laín *Antropología* 152–154).[5] They must work, moreover, against the uncertain deadlines of their own deaths. They do not know when they will die or what will become of them afterward. The human quest of self-creation thus consists of problematic, restless toil, compounded by anxiety resulting from fallibility and fragility in a world of uncertainty (Laín *Antropología* 152–155; Ortega, 1947: 33–35; Zubiri, 1986: 618–620; Zubiri, 1995: 262–263).

This structure of general ideas on living is applied to the cases of Castro and Silva, who sketch the human being's vain struggle for self-creation and meaning in this world of restlessness and uncertainty. Both portray the transformation human beings undergo during the course of their lives. They show that humans become more disillusioned as they grow older. The two authors contrast happy, innocent evocations of youth with their present world-weariness stemming from their accumulated experience. Both Silva and Castro clearly express a deep feeling of emptiness and a longing for a guiding principle to explain existence and to help humans live their lives. However, though they both desire religious faith, they are unable to overcome doubts. Silva believes that science has destroyed faith. Castro also deals with the same problem of science versus faith but unlike Silva never lets go of her hope of reconciling the two. Their feelings of aimlessness and confusion arise because they see the failures of both faith and science to explain existence and the essence of human nature.

Thus, Silva's and Castro's persistent anguish derives from a world inexplicable to human understanding. For them, reality consists of irrational suffering. Orjuela affirms that Silva's tendency to intellectualize existence makes him a skeptic, resulting in a sarcastic repudiation of religious faith (1976:111). Castro's inability to reconcile human suffering within the context of Catholicism causes her to lose her faith. Silva, like Castro, tragically shows how the human being yearns for meaning yet "sin esperanza, sigue con rumbo incierto en su búsqueda interminable, angustiosa e inútil" (Orjuela, 1976: 109, without hope, continues on an uncertain course in a never-ending, anguished, and futile search). Critics such as Mayoral (1974: 50–60), Kulp-Hill (36–37), Osiek (1978: 77), and Cuervo Márquez (504) indicate pessimistic themes that predominate in

Castro's and Silva's works, as when these writers painfully confront human mortality without discovering a transcendent purpose to life. This present study identifies the source of Castro's and Silva's disillusionment specifically as the uncertainty and deprivation inherent in existence. This work also examines the two authors' view of human life as radical insufficiency as it impacts on the form and content of their writing.

In chapter I, human restlessness appears contrasted with the immutability of objects as both authors describe how human beings become psychologically and spiritually disillusioned. Limitations on the human being's ability for self-creation receive careful analysis. Castro represents the restrictions imposed on nineteenth-century women writers, as well as the tragic results of forced Galician emigration. Silva describes how the deficient educational level of Colombian society limits artistic achievement. Both Castro and Silva reveal a poignant desire to evade the pain of everyday life through dreams, though this tendency is much more prevalent in Silva. However, both realize that their dreams are only temporary illusions that serve to underscore the inescapable radical deficiency of existence. Both writers deplore the lack of enduring values and norms that would give them security and meaning in life.

Chapter II focuses on art as a failed possibility for finding meaningfulness in life. Both authors reveal uncertainties toward the interpretation, judgment, creation, and permanence of art, especially of their own writing, because of personal and social constraints. Yet the very uncertainty inherent in life impels Castro and Silva to continue writing. The shadow leitmotif in their poetry is a vivid expression of their fear and anxiety in response to the insufficiencies of existence. Just as the shadow is the privation of light with a definite force in their lives, so Castro and Silva look at living as a privation with power to control their destinies.

Chapter III explores the uncertainty of love in these authors. For both love is an essential theme, yet love stays unfulfilled and unfulfillable because of the instability of human existence. Silva frequently shows how love ends in death. Castro reveals the pain of women who become widows of the living and the dead as their spouses depart, all victims of Galician emigration. The characters of the two authors often suffer in love because they have difficulty reconciling idealized versions of romantic love with daily experience.

Chapter IV concentrates on the theme of death as the limit of human endeavors and as another failed possibility of finding meaning in life. Both writers show the uncertainty of when and how death of the mind or body may strike and persistently question what occurs after biological death. They reveal that a hedonistic approach to life results in overwhelming feelings of emptiness. Castro and Silva depict death as the only means of escape from the inevitable pain and hardship of existence, despite their ambiguous attitudes toward the afterlife.

This work takes a new approach to Castro and Silva by thematically and stylistically analyzing the privative sense of life found in their works. The significance of these writers has transcended their own time and will increase if their work is examined in the context of authors and thinkers who succeeded them such as Ortega, Zubiri, and Laín. With moving sincerity and beauty Castro and Silva give anguished expression to suffering in an uncertain world and to the terrifying implications of human consciousness.

Chapter I

The Experience of Radical Insufficiency

Rosalía de Castro and José Asunción Silva express eternal concerns about the meaning of life and death, anticipating many themes of the existentialists. Both are writers in transition who lived in a century characterized by political chaos and ideological strife. In Spain conflict resulted as conservatives defended traditional values against the secular, progressive, and democratic trends arising in France, England, and elsewhere in the West (Kulp-Hill 15). Likewise, in Colombia the second half of the nineteenth century displayed social and religious upheaval. Tradition underwent challenge in a climate of increasing liberalism following the newly established federalist government of 1863. The influence of French and English philosophical and political ideas also contributed to the general turmoil in Colombia (Camacho Guizado, 1968: 13–14). Castro and Silva absorbed quite naturally these uncertainties and doubts, the political and religious rumblings of the times. They arrived at the disquieting realization that there is no absolute blueprint for life. Their works are permeated by anguish that relates to their feelings of abandonment in an uncertain world and their deep desire for guiding principles. Deploring the lack of enduring values and norms that would give life meaning, they consistently present the essential orphanhood of the human being. However, they do not offer solutions to the problem of existence because they believe that human beings can never discern the ultimate purpose for living. Neither philosophy, science, art, love, nor religion explain the world to them; their agony is born of the failure of human reason. Nevertheless, despite their anguish, they do not hide from their realization. Instead, they show that for human beings to comprehend reality, they must strip away the false, albeit comforting, preconceptions about life cherished for centuries. This chapter reveals how Castro and Silva, who once approached life from a conventional perspective, came to perceive being human as the experience of radical insufficiency.

The Restlessness of the Human Being

The Deluded Innocence of Childhood

Lacking a fixed nature, humans are dynamic beings that change continuously throughout their lives. Their mutability forms part of the restlessness of being human. For both Castro and Silva, this process of change seems inevitably to lead the human being from a state of seeming innocence and faith during childhood to one of disillusionment and uncertainty during adulthood.[1] Although Castro occasionally depicts the physical and mental suffering of children (*Follas novas* 368, 399 [New Leaves]; *Sar* 502–503; *La hija del mar* 130 [Daughter of the Sea]; *El primer loco* 729 [The First Madman]), both she and Silva generally perceive childhood as a deluded though contented state, that is, as a time when they believed in God and in the goodness of their fellow human beings, trusted in the attainability of hopes and dreams, and thought that life was meaningful. With maturity they come to see being human as radical insufficiency because human beings can never attain a state of pure innocence. In their writings Castro (*El caballero de las botas azules* 49 [The Gentleman of the Blue Boots]; *Flavio* 226) and Silva (*Libro de versos* 9, 12) emphasize the fleeting nature of youthful trustfulness. Castro affirms that unmitigated, unexplained suffering is what separates the world of the child from that of the adult: "La nieve de los años, de la tristeza el hielo/constante, al alma niegan toda ilusión amada,/todo dulce consuelo" (*Sar* 460–461, The snow of years, the ice of sadness/ever present, deny the soul cherished illusions,/every sweet consolation). In a thematically similar poem Castro's poetic voice describes the pain of knowing that she will witness her beloved childrens' inevitable transformation from innocence (though deluded) to disillusionment as they continue living. She uses much entrapment imagery to underscore the fact that a mother cannot protect her children from the disappointment that experience brings:

> Yo, en tanto, bañados mis ojos, les miro
> y guardo silencio, pensando:—En la tierra

¿adónde llevaros, mis pobres cautivos,
que no hayan de ataros las mismas cadenas?
Del hombre, enemigo del hombre, no puede
libraros, mis ángeles, la égida materna. (*Sar* 488)

I, meanwhile, with tears in my eyes, look upon them
and keep silent, thinking:—On earth
where to take you, my poor captives,
where the same chains will not imprison you?
From man, enemy of man, cannot
protect you, my angels, the maternal aegis.

Through her novelistic character Flavio, Castro powerfully illustrates how childhood ingenuousness is soon lost in the adult world. The overall theme of the novel is the corruption of innocence as a result of experience and contact with others. Soon after his parents die, twenty-year-old Flavio leaves his ancestral home, symbol of the womb and its protection. He sets forth on a journey of initiation. Significantly, Castro often refers to Flavio not by name but simply as "the traveler" (275). Coming on a nocturnal party, he is immediately mesmerized by its impressionistic beauty (234). The scene he witnesses foreshadows the changes that will take place in him. Society corrupts Flavio just as the party unnaturally taints the unspoiled landscape. The crash of Flavio's carriage after he leaves the party to continue his journey of discovery represents his fall from innocence into the world of disillusionment (275). Subsequently, at a masquerade party symbolizing the deceptive nature of reality, women deceive Flavio into thinking that his beloved Mara has been unfaithful. Freely partaking in the experiences of life, Flavio is then seduced by carnal love and materialism. For Mara, already distrustful and cynical at fifteen, Flavio's actions confirm her pessimism about human inconstancy. Flavio also disillusions Rosa, a young girl whom he seduces and then abandons with their child (463). Fully embracing a dissolute lifestyle, Flavio disparagingly equates his former innocence with a simpleminded conception of the world (463).

Silva similarly reveals how experience transforms childhood perceptions into undeceit. The grandmother of "Los maderos de San Juan" (The Wood of Saint John) is agonizingly aware that with maturity her grandchild will exchange innocence for disillusionment, just as she has:

Y en tanto en las rodillas cansadas de la Abuela
Con movimiento rítmico se balancea el niño
Y ambos conmovidos y trémulos están,

La Abuela se sonríe con maternal cariño
Mas cruza por su espíritu como un temor extraño
Por lo que en lo futuro, de angustia y desengaño
Los días ignorados del nieto guardarán. (*Libro de versos* 12)

And while on the tired knees of the grandmother,
With rhythmical movement the child rocks
And both moved and tremulous are,
The grandmother smiles with maternal love
But her soul is shaken as if by a strange fear
Of what in the future, of anguish and disillusionment
The unforseeable days of the grandchild will bring.

Usually, the child symbolizes the future, whereas the old represent the past. In Silva's poem, however, the grandmother is just as much a symbol of the future as of the past. As Silva interprets the grandmother's thoughts, he emphatically uses the future tense. Through her own accumulated suffering and subsequent pessimism she vividly portrays what her grandson's life and worldview will be like. Silva constantly returns to the alexandrines accented in -án, the knell of fatality. This -án is a derivative of the nursery rhyme, "Los maderos de San Juan" (The Wood of Saint John). Used as a refrain that fuses past, present, and future, the nursery rhyme acquires substantial depth to become, as the poem progresses, an almost sinister reminder of innocence and simplicity lost as the child matures. The nursery rhyme represents, then, through contrast, the lack of lighthearted exuberance and gaiety in adulthood. Another device Silva employs to emphasize his theme of disillusionment is repetition. The stanza quoted above, the penultimate, is exactly the same as the second stanza except for a slight variation in the first line. Not only does Silva deepen the pathos and contribute to the heavy and melancholic mood of the poem through this repetition, but he also eloquently creates the sensation of foreshadowing as to the child's ominous future. The child will only be able to recapture the happy past through memory as a disillusioned adult.

Nevertheless, both Castro and Silva view the deluded innocence of childhood more favorably than the disillusionment of adulthood. In "Padrón y las inundaciones" (Padrón and the Floods) Castro recalls the golden days of childhood and adolescence spent in the manor house when "la esperanza, ahora huida, andaba agitando entonces sus luminosas alas" (635, hope, now gone, would flutter then its luminous wings).With deep feelings of *saudade* Silva and Castro look back to childhood: "Feliz edad de plácidos engaños" (*Intimidades* 184, Happy age of blissful delusions

[Private Thoughts]).[2] Sensitively they portray human yearning for the lost paradise of childhood "por saberse constitutivamente, como hombre, *desterrado* de esta seguridad, en la que no se moría. Es por tanto, la saudade, una expresión biológico-afectiva de este ser-arrojado-en-el-mundo" (Rof Carballo 128, knowing themselves to be constitutively, as human beings, exiled from this security, in which one never dies. Therefore, *saudade* is a biological-affective expression of this being hurled into the world).

Silva in particular writes about the blend of fantasy and reality that makes childhood such a special state, as opposed to disillusioned adulthood (*Libro de versos* 8–9,14–16). Implicitly, he conceives childhood innocence as the candid acceptance of, and belief in, ultimate authority, both human and divine, as well as a lack of motivation to attempt a rational understanding of existence (*Libro de versos* 8–9). In this stage of life practical considerations are nonexistent, and the child organizes "horrísona batalla/En donde hacen las piedras de metralla/Y el ajado pañuelo de bandera" (*Libro de versos* 9, horrendous battle/In which stones serve as ammunition/And the crumpled handkerchief as a flag). Unwittingly the child imitates one of the horrible realities of adult life. In another poem Silva contrasts Bolívar's somber statue with the children who play at the foot of its pedestal: "Un idilio de vida sonrïente/Y de alegría fatua" (*Libro de versos* 18, An idyll of smiling life/And of inane happiness). He thus represents childhood innocence in juxtaposition to Bolívar as the incapacity to apprehend the suffering of others.

Silva repeatedly attempts to use memories of innocent childhood days, recaptured through the mists of time, as a psychological oasis.[3] He depicts images of turning inward, trying to dissociate himself from the disillusionment of adulthood: "Ansiosa el alma torna/A los felices días de la infancia/Que pasaron veloces" (*Intimidades* 181, Anxiously the soul returns/To the happy days of childhood/That swiftly passed). He wishes to supersede the suffering of life through memory: "Cómo es de dulce en horas de amargura/Dirigir al pasado la mirada" (*Libro de versos* 9, How sweet it is in bitter times/To turn one's gaze to the past). But sweet childhood memories can also cause pain as a stark reminder of a time forever lost. Adults can only evoke sadly "todo el poema triste de la remota infancia" (*Libro de versos* 12, the whole sad poem of long-gone childhood). Silva fully recognizes that "el pasado perfuma los ensueños" (*Libro de versos* 40, the past perfumes reveries). Time acts as an idealizing agent on a nebulous past and makes the present all the more unbearable. To Castro, however, memories of youth are distinctly painful because they emphasize the happiness now lacking in her life. Memory forms a source of unending anguish as she realizes that through remembrance human beings recognize their own restlessness (*Follas novas* 301–302). In one poem, for example, Castro uses gold leaves to symbolize an elusive treasure gone—the green of spring and summer and, by extension, youth and hope. Movingly, she indicates the pain she feels whenever she recalls the past: "¿Por qué tan terca,/tan fiel memoria me ha dado el cielo?" (*Sar* 480, Why such a stubborn,/such a faithful memory has heaven bestowed upon me?). Ultimately for Castro, memory is one more example of the cruelty and futility of life.

The Awareness and Disillusionment of Adulthood

Both Castro and Silva portray adulthood as a state of suffering and lost hopes. In the long reflective poem "Orillas del Sar" (Banks of the River Sar), Castro describes the increasing disillusionment that maturity brings. The poetic voice looks out the window, surveying a wavy sea of green trees. The trees, observed from a position of height and distance, symbolize gained experience and the greater perspective of age. The passage of time has influenced Castro's life in negative ways as the innocence of youth has given way to pessimism, which she views as a mature acceptance of the possibilities of life. Suggesting withdrawal from the world, the poetic voice speaks in the past tense about the forest once loved. The fluttering leaves reinforce the theme of the vicissitudes of human existence. The green of the leaves may represent the hope of youth, and the birds that dwell among them the lofty aspirations of youth. But the woodland and its symbolism appear utterly foreign now. Somber but resigned, the poetic voice calls attention to feelings of desolation. The ghosts, made more vivid by the adjective *white*, are the hopes and dreams of youth, which only haunt human beings:

Bajemos, pues, que el camino
antiguo nos saldrá al paso,
aunque triste, escabroso y desierto,
y cual nosotros cambiado,
lleno aún de las blancas fantasmas
que en otro tiempo adoramos. (*Sar* 459)

Let's go down, then, for the path
of old will come to meet us,
although sad, rugged and deserted,
changed like ourselves,
it is still filled with the white ghosts
that at another time we adored.

Silva also considers maturity as necessarily a symbol of disillusionment. He emphasizes the antipodal nature of youth and old age through juxtaposition in "La abulea y la nieta" (*Intimidades* 184–185, The Grandmother and the Granddaughter). Silva contrasts the granddaughter's white forehead with the grandmother's, darkened and whithered by heartache. The grandmother no longer experiences the hope that comes with each new day, as hope is the exclusive property of youth. Silva and Castro express that a consequence of suffering is often a hardening of the mental and emotional self toward others. Silva describes in "Perdida" (Lost) how an idealistic young girl, left pregnant and abandoned, becomes diseased and disillusioned as she avenges herself on all men (*Intimidades* 163–164). Likewise, as beggars are cruelly turned away from the home of one who was once a beggar himself, Castro tragically explains, "la miseria seca el alma/y los ojos además" (*Sar* 502, suffering dries the soul/and the eyes too).

To underscore their view that humans necessarily change as they mature, becoming more disillusioned over time, Castro and Silva contrast human mutability with such external and concrete items as statues, the seemingly fixed nature of the physical world, stories, nursery rhymes, and bells. In "Na catredal" (*Follas novas* 291–294, In the Cathedral), Castro's poetic voice expresses anguish at the loss of her previously intact religious beliefs. During a visit to a cathedral of younger days, she experiences feelings of spiritual orphanhood that heighten her sense of disorientation and inner change as she surveys the frozen statues she knew at a more innocent time in her life when her religious faith was strong. Observing the predominance of old people in various corners, Castro now views faith in its capacity to provide support to those who will soon face death. Matching her depressed mood is the organ that emits melancholy tones to which sad bells respond from afar. Castro's poetic voice notices how the statue of the Messiah seems still to be perspiring blood (291). Throughout her poem she utilizes the present tense to emphasize the continuous, unchanged physical environment of the cathedral in contrast to her evolving pessimism. Her frequent use of interrogatives and exclamations also conveys her anguish at change in herself, and repetition serves to highlight her nervousness. The predominance of *s* in the lines below (1, 2, 5, 7, 10) also suggests a privation of sound that reinforces her theme of emptiness in the wake of her loss of faith:

> ¡Como me miran eses calabres
> i aqueles deños!
> ¡Como me miran facendo moecas

dende as colunas onde os puxeron!
¿Será mentira, será verdade?
Santos do ceo,
¿saberán eles que son a mesma
daqueles tempos? ...
Pero xa orfa, pero enloitada,
pero insensibre cal eles mesmos ...
¡Como me firen! ... Voume, si, voume,
¡que teño medo! (*Follas novas* 293)

How these demons look at me
and those dead!
How they look at me grimacing
from the columns where they are!
Is it true, or is it a lie?
Saints in heaven,
do they know that I am the same one
of that time?
And now an orphan, and in mourning,
and insensible as they are ...
How they hurt me! ... I am going, yes, I am going,
for I am afraid!

Self-consciously she feels the statues are staring and grimacing at her, and she eloquently projects her fear and guilt at having lost her faith. The verticality of the cathedral columns represents an upward impulse, a deep desire for self-affirmation in the faith of her forebears. Columns also symbolize the stability lost along with faith. Toward the end of the poem, sunlight streaming on a high chandelier sheds reflections on the cathedral floor and produces dreams of religious illumination. Swiftly, however, the shadows of religious doubt appear and, once more, "todo é negrura, todo é misterio" (293, all is darkness, all is mystery). The poetic subject flees the cathedral in fear as now everything is a hurtful reminder of her pessimistic outlook about God's existence. Continuously Castro stresses that her problematic religious faith is the source of her prevailing sadness and confusion.

In another poem she contrasts the indifference of nature and eternal renewal to human beings, who inevitably change during the course of their lives. As critic Kathleen Kulp affirms, Castro "is preoccupied with irrevocable change and temporality, and the Heraclitean concept that man cannot step twice into the same stream" (186). In the poem "¡ Adios!" (Good-bye) her poetic voice describes how she leaves home as "os vaiviéns da fertuna/pra lonxe me arrastran" (*Follas novas* 289, the ups and downs of fortune/drag me far away). Before departing, she pensively surveys the town cathedral and surrounding countryside. She emphasizes, on an uncertain future return, that nature and the cathedral will remain the same, but the people she has left behind will be different. She measures this transformation in terms of the misfortunes they will have endured (289). Castro's depictions of the painful changes and transformations that the human being undergoes caused her husband Manuel Murguía to comment that "los montes que ve desde su ventana son los mismos que veía en otros tiempos; todo es igual: sólo que faltan alrededor suyo algunos seres, y en su corazón muchas esperanzas; sólo ella, siendo la misma, es distinta" (1944: 155, the mountains she sees from her window are the same she saw in the past; everything is the same: but missing are some persons around her, and many hopes in her heart; only she, while the same, is different).

In other poems Castro compares the human being's changefulness with the changes in nature. She likens the dissolution of clouds to the dissolution of youthful dreams and hopes. Clouds, always in a state of metamorphosis, convey well the mutability of the human being as time passes (*Follas novas* 290). In another poem, seeing some flowers and stars that seem to be the same as ones she had known when she was younger and had strong faith in God, Castro's poetic voice notes that in reality the flowers and stars are different, just as she is different: she is less innocent. The awareness of how she has changed is a source of deep sorrow:

> Alma que vas huyendo de ti misma,
> ¿qué buscas, insensata, en las demás?
> Si secó en ti la fuente del consuelo,
> secas todas las fuentes has de hallar.
> ¡Que hay en el cielo estrellas todavía,
> y hay en la tierra flores perfumadas!
> ¡ Sí! ... Mas no son ya aquellas
> que tú amaste y te amaron, desdichada. (*Sar* 479)

> *Soul in flight from yourself,*
> *what do you expect, fool, to find in others?*
> *If the spring of consolation dried up in you,*
> *dried up all other springs you will find.*
> *There are still stars in the sky,*
> *and on earth scented flowers!*
> *Yes! ... But they are not those*
> *that you loved and that loved you, wretched one.*

She writes the poem in hendecasyllables except for line 7, which is heptasyllabic, thereby reinforcing the brevity of all things, even of those that may appear eternal. Her self-deprecatory tone implies that she should be well aware of negative change in herself. In a thematically similar poem daisies that grow amid the green grass symbolize lost naiveté and youthful resilience. The tone of the first three stanzas of the poem is calm and hopeful. But as seasons pass her poetic voice contrasts the flowers' apparent changelessness with her own variability (*Sar* 508–509).

Like Castro, Silva mourns human mutability. In "Crepúsculo" (Twilight), he contrasts human transformations with the archetypal permanence of children's stories (*Libro de versos* 14–16). The unvarying dodecasyllabic rhythm and consonant rhyme of this poem additionally emphasize the persistence of beloved storybooks through memory in disenchanted adulthood. In "Los maderos de San Juan" (The Wood of Saint John) Silva also contrasts an unchanging nursery rhyme with the tragic changes the human being experiences (*Libro de versos* 11–13). In "Día de difuntos" (Day of the Dead), he pessimistically juxtaposes the solemn bells that ring eternally for the dead with the brittle, crystalline voice of the hour bell that flippantly measures the inconstancy of human sentiment:

> Y hay algo angustioso e incierto
> Que mezcla a ese sonido su sonido,
> E inarmónico vibra en el concierto
> Que alzan los bronces al tocar a muerto,
> Por todos los que han sido! (*Libro de versos* 65)
>
> *And there is something anguished and uncertain,*
> *That adds to that sound its own,*
> *And inharmoniously rings in the chorus*
> *Of the bells that ring for the dead,*
> *For all those who have been!*

Silva ruefully affirms that loved ones who have passed away remain but a day in the memory of the living. He reinforces the fugacity of memory through metrical variation. Yet he also employs repetition of lines, words, and even rhythms at various points to contrast the persistent tolling of bells with the painful recognition of human change, implicitly including his own, from innocence to disillusionment.

Bells that evoke awareness of a more innocent conception of life also peal in Castro's poetry and often inspire acute feelings of *saudade* (*Cantares gallegos* 529–532, 541–543, [Galician Songs]; *Follas novas* 289, 291, 314; *Sar* 458, 514). In "O toque da alba" (The Ringing of the Bells at Dawn) her poetic voice describes the sad, grave tone of a cathedral bell and recalls how, when young, she had awakened to the ringing with hopeful anticipation. But now this constant sound is a distressing gauge of psychological change. Through apostrophe she pathetically wonders to what end the bell brings painful awareness of personal maturation. She concludes her poem by ascribing to the bell a continuity that will transcend her own final transformation: "Mais ben pronto ... ben pronto, os meus oídos/nin te oirán na tarde nin na aurora" (*Follas novas* 302, But very soon ... very soon, my ears/will not hear you at dusk or at dawn). Through repetition of verses, as well as the steady rhythm of heptasyllables and hendecasyllables, Castro stylistically reinforces regularity and continuity, as represented by the bell vis-à-vis recognition of her present pessimism.

Clearly Poe's "The Bells" (20–23) influenced Castro's "O toque da alba" (*Follas novas* 301–302), "Las campanas" (*Sar* 537), and Silva's "Día de difuntos" (*Libro de versos* 64–68). Each of these writers symbolically contrasts the permanence of sounding bells with the mutable, changing human being who lives and suffers in an unpredictable world. In the case of all three authors their poems were written toward the end of their careers and are thus enriched by life experience. In his poem Poe describes four kinds of bells that swing at different periods of human life; there are sleigh bells that represent youthful innocence, wedding bells that supposedly foretell future happiness, alarm bells that relate directly to the uncertainty of existence, and funeral bells, which signify death with all of its philosophical and fearful implications. From a technical standpoint Castro's and Silva's poems also resemble "The Bells." Poe varies his meter to fit his sequence of themes and employs repetition, consonant rhyme, and onomatopoeia to build a crescendo of sound that imitates the bells that terrifyingly symbolize, as in Castro and Silva, the irrevocable flow of time. Another similarity of these poems is that the authors project human voices or attitudes on the bells. Such identification signals their impossible desire to reconcile the durability of the bells with the instability of humans, as well as their need to discover the very purpose of existence in their consciousness of the passage of time.

Limitations on the Human Being's Ability for Self-Creation

Castro and Silva suggest that the uncertain struggle for self-creation is part of what leads to the disillusionment of adulthood. They recognize with sadness that although human beings have the potential to become and do many things, they do not have infinite potential. Specifically the authors depict the limitations that society and personal circumstances impose on human beings as they try to choose and fulfill their life projects. Castro feels restricted by social attitudes toward women authors and uses her writings to expose such injustice. She also reveals the tragic results in human terms of forced Galician emigration. Silva, for his part, depicts not only the horrors of poverty (though much less insistently than Castro) but also the artistic, cultural, and intellectual constraints of Colombian bourgeois society.

Castro: Limitations Because of Gender

As critic Marina Mayoral accurately affirms, "Rosalía, en el prólogo a *La hija del mar*, se refiere muy claramente a las limitaciones que el ser mujer impone a una escritora" (*Actas*, 1986: 342, Rosalía, in the prologue to *Daughter of the Sea*, refers very clearly to the limitations that being a woman imposes upon a female writer).[4] In this prologue Castro excuses and justifies her "pecado inmenso e indigno de perdón" (47, immense sin unworthy of forgiveness) of having produced a book. She cites men such as Feijóo, who have supported the intellectual pursuits of women, and then names successful women who have gained fame for their political, religious, and artistic endeavors, such as Joan of Arc, Saint Teresa de Jesus, and George Sand. Castro ends her prologue with a powerful indictment of a society that tragically limits women in expressing themselves affectively and intellectually (48). In the prologue to *Follas novas* she adopts a pose of humility to soften negative public and critical response to a supposedly unfeminine inquiry into metaphysics. In an attempt to undermine censorship she belittles her capacity as a woman to formulate profound thought: "O pensamento da muller é lixeiro, góstanos como ás borboletas, voar de rosa en rosa, sobre as cousas tamén lixeiras; non é feito para nós o duro traballo da meditación" (*Follas novas* 270, The thoughts of women are light, thus like butterflies, we like to fly from rose to rose, over the lightest of things; not for us the arduous task of thinking). After this subtle opening, however, she proceeds to challenge furtively patriarchal society and its preconceived notions about female writing in the brief opening poem. Her challenge is in the form of an unanswered question. She affirms that she does not sing of doves and flowers, yet she is a woman:

> Daquelas que cantan as pombas i as frores
> todos din que teñen alma de muller,
> pois eu que n'as canto, Virxe da Paloma,
> ¡ai!, ¿de que a terei? (*Follas novas* 277)
>
> *Of those who sing of doves and flowers*
> *it is said that they have the soul of woman,*
> *I do not sing of them, most sainted Virgin,*
> *oh!, what is mine [soul] like?*

Doves and flowers represent acceptable female discourse in Castro's time, discourse consisting of the sentimental, the beautiful, and, of course, the insubstantial. Though a woman, Castro affirms that she prefers quite naturally to explore more meaningful topics. Castro herself was more fortunate than most women as she wrote with the approval and encouragement of her husband.[5] Critic Janet Pérez notes that Castro "probably experienced diminished literary discrimination thanks to Murguía's support" (33).

In *Lieders* (Songs) and *Las literatas* (Literary Women) Castro assumes a more forceful pose and passionately censures social constraints on women. She exclaims in *Lieders* that "el patrimonio de la mujer son los grillos de la esclavitud" (41, the patrimony of woman are the shackles of slavery).[6] Under the guise of reading a letter (the *Carta a Eduarda* [Letter to Eduarda]) that she finds while walking on the outskirts of the city, Castro is able to reveal more directly the unfair treatment of women writers by society.[7] She divulges how the female author is the object not only of masculine but also of feminine derision: "Las mujeres ponen en [*sic!*] relieve hasta el más escondido de tus defectos y los hombres no cesan de decirte ... que una mujer de talento es una verdadera calamidad, que vale más casarse con la burra de Balaam" (*Las literatas* 657–658, Women bring to the fore the most hidden of your defects and men do not stop telling you ... that a talented woman is a real misfortune, that it is better to wed the ass of Balaam). She describes how male writers think that women should attend to more feminine pursuits, such as mending their husband's socks if they have a husband and if not "aunque sean los del criado" (658, even those of the manservant), in this way reinforcing their lowly status and inconsequential purpose in life. Castro's testimony, undeniably referring to herself, exposes how the existing patriarchal system convinces women that writing is incompatible with the true measure of their worth, which lies in the conscientious execution of domestic duties:

> Cosa fácil era para algunas abrir el armario y plantarle delante de las narices los zurcidos pacientemente trabajados, para probarle que el escribir algunas páginas no le hace a todas olvidarse de sus quehaceres domésticos, pudiendo añadir que los que tal murmuran saben olvidarse, en cambio, de que no han nacido más que para tragar el pan de cada día y vivir como los parásitos. (658)
>
> *It was easy for some to open the closet and thrust under their noses the patiently worked darnings, to prove that writing some pages does not make all women forgo their domestic chores, and could even add that those who so gossip know how to forget, on the other hand, that they were not born only to consume their daily bread and live like parasites.*

Injustice in any form angered Castro and is evident above in her disparaging tone. She creates an alter ego in her character Mara (*Flavio*), a young woman who feels social pressure and struggles pathetically to justify her literary vocation to herself. Poignantly Castro describes how Mara, out of shame, needs to hide her verses, "cuyos renglones ella hubiera preferido borrar quizá con su propia sangre antes de que un ojo profano detuviese en ellos su imprudente mirada" (299, whose lines she would have preferred to erase perhaps with her own blood rather than have a profane eye scan them with its imprudent glance). Mara reflects the attitudes of society concerning "correct" female behavior, which precludes expressing thoughts and true emotions in written form.

In *El caballero de las botas azules* (The Gentleman of the Blue Boots) Castro points out an important reason why women's potential is limited from the start. In the character of Dorotea she reveals that the prevailing mindset of educators is that it is actually their duty to provide an inferior education to young women.[8] Satirically, Castro depicts the proud Dorotea's conversation with Melchor, the young sexton engaged to Dorotea's niece and charge, Mariquita. Dorotea prides herself in preserving Mariquita's intellectual and worldly ignorance, presenting it as an asset to her future spouse: "Eso sí; no sabe nada de nada y no como otras, que en todo quieren meterse y aprender lo que no les conviene. ... Cieguita la tengo, como un gatito recien nacido" (59, Rather she knows nothing about anything not like others, who would have a hand in everything and learn what is not good for them to know. ... Blind I keep her, like a newborn kitten). With typical fair-mindedness Castro represents Dorotea as an obscurantist who fervently opposes a man, fellow schoolteacher Ricardito Majón, arguing for a liberal education for young women (184).

Castro thus shows that women share some of the blame for their lack of intellectual freedom, as they sometimes condemn their own gender to ignorance.

Limitations Because of Poverty

Silva, like Castro, portrays how circumstances may impede self-realization. He describes, for instance, the limits that poverty imposes on the human being's potential by showing the inevitable fate of poor women of the time.[9] He depicts an impoverished young woman who, left pregnant and abandoned, bitterly descends into a life of prostitution (*Intimidades* 163–164). His wealthy protagonist walks through poor London neighborhoods, observing the "caras marchitas de chicuelas desvergonzadas, corroídas ya por el vicio, y que tienen todavía aire de inocencia no destruida por la incesante venta de sus pobres caricias inhábiles" (*De sobremesa* 279, worn faces of shameless young girls, corrupted already by vice, who still keep an air of innocence not destroyed by the incessant selling of their poor, clumsy caresses [*After-Dinner Chat*]). In "El Recluta" (The Recruit) Silva also represents how a poor man is drafted into the army and dies tragically. His mother leads, as he did before, a meaningless life in her poverty (*Poesías varias* 104–105 [*Miscellaneous Poems*]). It is important to remember, however, that although Silva sympathizes with the poor, he does not identify with the poor in his writings as Castro does. He describes their plight from an aristocratic distance. Castro, on the other hand, most closely associated with the humble folk and was always very conscious of the social aspect of her work.

In relating to the poor Castro particularly praises the nobleness of those who suffer in silence (*Follas novas* 407).[10] Through her poetic adaptation of a Galician story about an orphan who reaches adulthood in abject poverty and must beg for a living, Castro illustrates how poverty dehumanizes and limits possibilities for self-affirmation because "donde houbera/pobreza, e soledade e desventura,/groira, dicha e querer correndo pasan" (*Cantares gallegos* 582, where there is poverty, loneliness and misfortune,/glory, happiness and love flee [*Galician Songs*]).[11] The slaughter of a pig, in which Vidal does not participate, represents the good living, which lies beyond the poor (*Cantares gallegos* 584).

In particular, Castro describes how her impoverished, unemployed Galician countrymen often had to seek work in other areas of Spain or Portugal, as well as in Latin America.[12] Poverty robs Galicians of the possibility of staying in their beloved homeland:

¡Van a deixa-la patria! ...
Forzoso, mais supremo sacrificio.
A miseria está negra en torno deles,
¡ai!, i adiante está o abismo! ... (*Follas novas* 406)

They are going to leave the homeland! ...
Necessary, supreme sacrifice.
The most abject misery surrounds them,
oh!, before them is the abyss! ...

Exclamations convey the intensity of Castro's empathy. The unjust and arbitrary aspects of forced emigration unquestionably influenced her view of existence. In answer to poet Ventura Ruiz Aguilera's query as to whether the Galician bagpipe sings or cries, Castro unhesitantly responds, as she thinks of the Galician emigres, "eu podo decirche:/Non canta, que chora" (*Cantares gallegos* 605, I can say to you: It does not sing, rather it cries). In this poem Castro describes not only how the poverty-stricken Galicians must leave a land that cannot sustain them but also how the rest of Spain has tragically forgotten Galicia. Castro continually depicts Galicia as the abandoned child of Spain, battling the perception "que Galicia é o rincón máis despreciable da terra" (*Cantares gallegos* 490, that Galicia is the most despicable corner of the earth). Metaphorically she links Galicia to her prevailing theme of orphanhood because of the mass exodus of its men: "Galicia, sin homes quedas/que te poidan traballar./Tés, en cambio, orfos e orfas" (*Follas novas* 407, Galicia, you are left without men/to work the land./You are left with orphans). She particularly comments on the distressing results of emigration on women and children (*El primer loco* 684 [The First Madman]). Castro also expresses anguish at the fact that even when poor Galicians attempt to better their lot by emigrating to places where work is available, they do not always succeed. She emphasizes the anxiety caused by this uncertainty as she compares the Galician emigrants to doves driven away from their native nest by the fox and kite: Galicians leave their homeland to aid their families, perhaps only to find withered fruit in other plains (*Sar* 491). In addition to describing these physical hardships, Castro also conveys the psychological impact of emigration and the acute loneliness it engenders as spouses, fathers, brothers, and sons depart. She describes with sadness how physical subsistence becomes the primary objective of life and denies personal fulfillment. Perhaps, as critic Rof Carballo maintains, Castro's own lack of a father image when she was growing up allows her to express with greater artistic depth the pain of the widows of the living and the dead: "La ausencia del padre, emigrado muchas veces, es un factor nada menospreciable en la constitución del alma galaica. La niña no tiene 'imago paternal,' núcleo viril sobre el que cristalizar lo más profundo de su ser" (121, The absence of the father, often an emigrant, is a factor not to be discounted in the formation of the Galician soul. The little girl lacks a father image, manly nucleus on which to crystallize the deepest part of her being).[13]

Limitations Because of Society

As with Castro, Silva reveals constraints to self-actualization. Particularly he points out the circumscription he experiences in Colombian bourgeois society. Through his characters, especially José Fernández, his alter ego (Orjuela, 1976: 19), he expresses the intellectual and cultural void that exists among the general public and seriously limits motivation and personal achievement. Fernández categorically renounces "la vida burguesa sin emociones y sin curiosidades" (*De sobremesa* 233, middle-class life without emotions and interests), which he perceives as mediocre and vulgar. Cynically he explains to friends, who insist he not squander his literary talents, that readers lack apperception and sensitivity to appreciate his poems.[14] In a voice that becomes increasingly vehement Fernández asks his friend Saenz, "¿Ya no recuerdas el artículo de Andrés Ramírez en que me llamó asqueroso pornógrafo y dijo que mis versos eran una mezcla de agua bendita y de cantáridas? Pues esa suerte correría el poema que escribiera" (236, Don't you remember anymore the article of Andrés Ramírez in which he called me a disgusting pornographer and said that my verses were a mixture of holy water and blisters? The same fate would await any I poem I were to write). While thinking about the essence of life, Fernández poignantly expresses his sense of isolation (233). He stands apart from other characters because he cannot accept, as they do, the incoherence and mystery of life. Yet ultimately, he gives up his search for impossible answers to existence, as well as his art, which so few understand. According to Dr. Charvet, he must live simply and without questions if he is to lead a normal life (314).

Similarly, in his poem "El mal del siglo" (*Gotas amargas* 74, *"Mal du siécle"* [Bitter Drops]), Silva describes how a patient's statements of alienation fall on the deaf ears of a doctor who, like the doctors in *De sobremesa* (285, 314), attends mainly to the body without penetrating the deeper sources of human malaise, such as the clash between the sensitive, intelligent human being with the mediocrity and harshness of society. The patient's reflections about life, his feelings of hopeless maladjustment, and his obvious learning contrast with the superficial remedy of the doctor for his depression. The dialogic format of the poem further opposes patient and doctor. Through the doctor Silva exposes the intellectual deficiency of a society filled with easy solutions, which concentrates wholly on the physical rather than on the philosophical aspects of life. Melancholy, boredom, and disillusionment characterize the patient's malady, which parallels the world-weariness of the early French romantics, who suffered the *mal de siécle*. The patient resembles the young philosopher of "Psicopatía" (*Libro de versos* 58–60, Mental Disorder), as both characters' fruitless reflections on life ultimately lead them to despair and prevent their social integration. Through the ignorant doctor Silva criticizes a society that feels threatened in its mediocrity by the philosopher's intellectualization of life. Indeed, society treats the introspective philosopher as if diseased and punishes him with ostracism.[15]

The Human Being's Inability to Escape Limitations

Acknowledging the insufficiency of human life, Castro and Silva thematically represent a desire to escape the limitations of existence. The contemplative tendency to embellish everyday life through dreams, the aspiration to elevate reality to a higher plane, to transform the real into the ideal, is consistent throughout Castro's and Silva's works. Through the image of soaring, Castro represents a human being's dream of transcending the baseness of existence:

> Mas aun sin alas cree o sueña que cruza el aire, los espacios,
> y aun entre el lodo se ve limpio, cual de la nieve el copo blanco. (*Sar* 500)
>
> *Even without wings she believes or dreams that she flies through the air, through space,*
> *and even in the mud she imagines herself clean, as the snowflake is white.*

Because of the inadequacies of life, Castro shows how the frightened human being may choose to live in a partial dream world as a means of psychological survival: "Astros y fuentes y flores, no murmuréis de mis sueños;/sin ellos, ¿cómo admiraros, ni cómo vivir sin ellos?" (*Sar* 519, Stars and fountains and flowers, do not whisper about my dreams;/without them, how to admire you or how to live without them?). However, she also represents an awareness of dreaming at a very conscious level; she is no longer a child who confuses the realms of dreams and reality (*Sar* 488). She sees her graying hair and the frost in the fields yet continues to envision the eternal spring of life (*Sar* 519). Dreams allow Castro to preserve some of the fresh hopefulness of youth. However, despite this tendency to drift into make-believe worlds (*Follas novas* 361–362; *Sar* 466, 487–488, 489–490, 499–500, 501, 519), the rational prevails in her works because she wishes to expose the radical insufficiency of being human. Most urgently, she wishes to portray the harshness of daily life for women and children living in an impoverished land (*Cantares gallegos* 555–556, 557–561, 598–601; *Follas novas* 272, 299, 306, 368–369, 374–376, 399, 407, 414–415, 428–429, 437–438; *Sar* 493, 502–503). Her conceptual imagery often supports stylistically a poetic vision directed firmly to this world. In fact, she shows how angst can arise from the violent juxtaposition of the human being's dream with the strictures of reality: "siempre a soñar condenado,/nunca puede sosegar" (*Sar* 501, always condemned to dream,/never at rest).

By contrast, Silva typically employs the realistic only for shock effect, as in the closing lines of "Psicopatía" (*Libro de versos* 60). He generally expresses the wish to avoid a reality he consistently depicts as cruel and which he cannot change (*Libro de versos* 8–9, 27, 50, 76–77; *Intimidades* 129, 131, 134, 137, 142, 148–150, 154–155, 161–162, 165, 167, 181, 201–202, 203, 207). Although both he and Castro at times portray dreaming as a technique for adapting to existence, the boundary between dreams and life is more clearly defined in Castro than in Silva. Indeed, Silva's "Futura" (Future) is a criticism of a society that rejects the dreamy idealism of Don Quixote (*Gotas amargas* 82–83, [Bitter Drops]). Although Silva's authorship of "Nidos" (Nests) is still unconfirmed, the imagery and conclusion certainly are characteristic of Silva: "¡Descansad en el mundo de los sueños/Y en la calma infinita de las cosas!" (Orjuela, 1990: 221, Rest in the world of dreams/And the infinite calm of things!). In "Las noches del hogar" (Nights at Home) Silva reinforces his theme of desiring refuge from the "movible océano" (*Intimidades* 162, moving ocean), that is, the unstable world. There is the sense in these verses that Silva's poetic voice wishes to hide from the pain of life and shield his identity from society at large. Silva's simile likening the conch to a home, symbolic of the womb, and pearls to humans inside the womb expresses another more subtle view of his psyche and, by extension, of his writing. When a foreign substance, like a grain of sand or a parasite, enters the body of a mollusk, the nacre-forming cells cover the invading substance until the foreign body is enclosed, and the pearl comes into being. The pearl is therefore the product of something completely isolated, independent, and removed. Silva's writings, like exquisite pearls, are a tangible attempt to insulate himself from a world that was a constant irritant. Silva usually represents life in his poetry in more impressionistic terms than Castro. Whenever reality pierces too deeply, he attempts to reach above it, creating worlds of softer contours. He fills his writing with insulated interiors and muted lights that implicitly reveal a longing for the softness lacking in his own frenetic life (*De sobremesa* 229).

In many of Silva's works the beauty of life is relegated to dreams. Through dreams, for instance, he represents a desire to achieve idealized romantic intimacy with women in faraway, fictionalized settings. While listening to his beloved play the piano, Silva's poetic voice imagines a scene in which both are suddenly transported to a Gothic castle, he as a blond page and she as a noblewoman (*Libro de versos* 27). Silva's alter ego, his novelistic protagonist José Fernández, also engages in dreamy reverie. He fantasizes about the deceased Russian writer and artist María Bashkirtseff, romantically delineating a feminine counterpart of himself (*De sobremesa* 241). When he first sees Helena Scilly Dancourt, the fifteen-year-old who becomes his amorous obsession, he also slips away to a realm of illusion as he visualizes the two of them together (*De sobremesa* 272). When Helena and her father leave with no forwarding address, Fernández embarks on a relentless but futile search as he pursues her image around the world. His physician Dr. Rivington insists that Fernández look for the real Helena, not the vision he has created (*De sobremesa* 287). Rivington warns Fernández that "el sueño es un veneno para usted" (*De sobremesa* 298, dreaming is poisonous for you). Silva is clearly aware that persistent dreaming in which life and people are idealized (to relieve psychological pressure in contact with bitter reality) can lead to permanent maladjustment. He shows that the contrast between the real and the imagined ends inevitably in painful disillusionment. In the case of his novelistic protagonist fantasy and reality become inextricably fused, and Fernández is therefore incapable of enjoying a fulfilling existence.

Silva also portrays the dangers of becoming too immersed in dreams in his poem "Lentes ajenos" (*Gotas amargas* 76–77, Borrowed Spectacles). Here he presents the schizophrenic Juan de Dios, who utilizes books to avoid engaging fully in life. From a young age Juan de Dios imitates various literary characters with his own lovers. Such excessive imagining prevents him from ever experiencing meaningful love with another human being or establishing a happy, integrated family life. Although acknowledging the temporary regenerative power of dreaming that sustains Juan de Dios, in the poetic sequel, "Cápsulas" (*Gotas amargas* 78, Capsules), Silva graphically underscores the danger of living in a dream world; when real suffering penetrates the fragile shield, the human being remains defenseless. When love and life become painful to Juan de Dios and he has no recourse to honest and open communication with other human beings, because of inability to communicate, he commits suicide in his extreme isolation (*Gotas amargas* 78).

More often than Castro, Silva contrasts the beauty and tenderness of dreams with reality in order to express more vividly the tragedy of human life:

> Mas cuando el alma en sus ensueños flota,
> La realidad asoma de improviso
> No más resuena la encantada nota....
> Brotan espinas do la rosa brota,
> Y en crüel se torna el paraíso. (*Intimidades* 149)
>
> *When the soul floats on dreams,*
> *Reality suddenly intrudes*
> *No more can the enchanted note be heard....*
> *Thorns spring where the rose blossoms,*
> *And there is cruelty in paradise.*

The rose symbolizes a fragile dream, the thorns the harshness of life. Acknowledging the perils of dreaming, however, Silva recognizes in his "Prólogo al poema intitulado 'Bienaventurados los que lloran' de Rivas Frade" (Prologue to the Poem Entitled "Blessed Are Those Who Cry" by Rivas Frade) that certain people are more prone to dreaming and introspection than others. In explaining the spiritual affinity between writers Rivas Frade, Heine, Bécquer, José Angel Porras, and Antonio Escobar, he could easily have been writing about himself:

> Todos esos poetas son espíritus delicadísimos y complicados a quienes su misma delicadeza enfermiza ahuyenta de las realidades brutales de la vida e imposibilita para encontrar en los amores fáciles y en las felicidades sencillas la satisfacción de sus deseos; a quienes lastiman a cada paso las piedras del camino y las durezas de los hombres, y que se refugian en sus sueños. (366)
>
> *All these poets are very delicate and complicated spirits whose same sickly sensitivity keeps them from the brutal realities of life and makes*

> *it impossible for them to find in easy love and simple happiness the satisfaction of their desires; they are constantly hurt by the pebbles on their path and the roughness of men, and take refuge in their dreams.*

Many critics claim that Silva also took refuge from reality by creating his character José Fernández, whom Silva consistently portrays as eluding prosaic reality.[16] Fernández is high-born, handsome, and wealthy, and he possesses superior literary talent. As critic Rafael Maya affirms:

> El gran sueño frustrado del poeta iba a cobrar vida espléndida por medio de la creación artística. *De sobremesa* es la novela de la evasión y de la compensación. De la evasión, porque le permitió a Silva sustraerse metódicamente a las vulgares necesidades que lo acuciaban, en días verdaderamente amargos, y de la compensación, porque vivió sus mejores sueños en la figura de su protagonista, que estaba modelado con los mas amplios toques de la imaginación creadora. (101–102)
>
> *The great frustrated dream of the poet was going to take splendid life through artistic creation.* After-Dinner Chat *is a novel of evasion and compensation. Evasion because it allowed Silva methodically to separate himself from the crass and vulgar needs that haunted him, in truly bitter days, and compensation, because he lived his best dreams in the person of his protagonist, construed with the most ample strokes of creative imagination.*

Castro and Silva also recognize elements of dreaming in the composition of human society itself, such as in the affirmation of an Afterlife. Reflecting on human longing for immortality, Castro wistfully writes, "Mas ¿quién sabe si en tanto hacia su fin caminan,/como el hombre, los astros con ser eternos sueñan?" (*Sar* 497, But who knows if as they move toward their end,/like man, the stars dream of being eternal?). Gazing at stars once adored by the Magi, Silva expresses a similar yearning without possibility of a cosmic response from the stars: "¿Por qué os calláis si estáis vivas/Y por qué alumbráis si estáis muertas?..." (*Libro de versos* 44, Why are you silent if you are alive/And why do you give off light if you are dead?..."). The ellipsis, a privation, speaks eloquently as the words themselves. Castro's desire for immortality anthropomorphizes the cosmos, whereas Silva's longing clashes with his skepticism produced by science. Castro's experience has also taught her that her view of truth as something divine and pure is nothing but a dream, another deception, in the emptiness of existence. She describes how clouds, constantly changing, symbolize the inexistence of an immutable higher truth (*Sar* 481). At times she indicates the hollowness of dreams (*Sar* 501). Silva similarly refers to daydreams as empty (*Libro de versos* 27). Nevertheless, both authors realize that dreams are poignant testimonies to the brutal, uncertain struggle of life, provoking the need for such mental and emotional separation. Whereas Castro suggests that dreams help prevent succumbing to despair, the disparity between dreams and life ultimately leads Silva to despair.

The Lack of Guiding Principles in Human Life

Castro and Silva express deep feelings of emptiness and a longing for guiding principles to explain human existence and to help them live their lives. They especially reveal a desire for religious guidance that resembles a thirst in its intensity. Castro herself repeatedly uses the image of thirst (*Follas novas* 283, 294, 314–315, 415; *Sar* 461, 471–472, 479, 499–500, 500–501). In one poem she compares the blistering sands on the beach, untouched by the cool waves, to her soul, which thirsts for immortality among the seraphims (*Sar* 471–472). Silva also views human worship of an untenable God as a quenchless thirst, though in a more characteristically sarcastic vein:

> Tiene instantes de intensas amarguras
> la sed de idolatrar que al hombre agita,
> del Supremo Señor la faz bendita
> ya no ríe del cielo en las alturas. (*Poesías varias* 115)
>
> *There are moments of intense bitterness*
> *the thirst of adoration that incites man,*
> *of the Supreme Lord the blessed face*
> *does not laugh from the height of heaven.*

Nevertheless, although Castro and Silva deeply wish to believe in God, their uncertainty yields anxiety. Religious doubt prevents them from accepting Catholic doctrine unconditionally as they would like and is a further testimony to the sincerity of their religious struggle. Silva describes the human being's journey in faith as uncertain, but he ultimately considers the likelihood of an afterlife in pessimistic terms:

Sin columna de luz, que en el desierto
guíe su paso a punto conocido,
continua el crüel peregrinaje,

para encontrar en el futuro incierto
las soledades hondas del olvido
tras las fatigas del penoso viaje. (*Poesías varias* 115)

Without a ray of light in the desert
to guide his steps to a known destination,
the cruel pilgrimage continues,

to find in the uncertain future
the deep solitude of oblivion
after the weariness of the hard journey.

The column of light is very like a reference to the pillar of fire with which God led the Israelites by night toward the Promised Land (Exod. 13:22). The privation of light Silva describes indicates, therefore, the lack of a tangible spiritual presence in the emptiness of life. The sonnet format may also relate to an underlying human need for structure. In a thematically similar poem, "... *?* ..." (*Libro de versos* 44), Silva also refers to the agonizing limitations of human knowledge. The poetic voice tenderly probes the immensity and mystery of the universe while gazing at stars that shine in the night. The stars may symbolize Silva's spiritual struggle, that is, his unsuccessful search for religious illumination in the darkness of human existence. Silva emphasizes how the stars shed no light on the meaning of life. There is not even the promise of daylight, which would indicate possible enlightenment in the future. The ellipses before and after the interrogative may signify the lack of understanding about the beginning and end of existence. The question Silva delicately poses at the conclusion of the poem expresses a deep desire for intercommunication between the human being and the cosmos. Yet life is in essence an unanswered and unanswerable question.

For Silva religious faith belongs to the past. He represents a society utterly lacking in Christian ethics, in which prostitution, adultery, and violence are rampant, signaling a lack of fear of divine retribution (*Intimidades* 163–164; *De sobremesa* 255, 279, 334, 342). His own loss of religious faith is a source of deep personal sorrow. He contrasts how in the past the ancient Romans sought relief and solace from the emptiness of life through their belief in Christ but how today science has destroyed that faith among people:

> La fe ciega que en su regazo de sombra les ofrecía una almohada donde descansar las cabezas a los cansados de la vida, ha desaparecido del universo. El ojo humano al aplicarlo al lente del microscopio que investiga lo infinitesimal y al lente del enorme telescopio que, vuelto hacia la altura, le revela el cielo, ha encontrado, arriba y abajo, en el átomo y en la inconmensurable nebulosa, una sola materia, sujeta a las mismas leyes que nada tienen que ver con la suerte de los humanos. (*De sobremesa* 335-336)
>
> *Blind faith which on its shadowy lap offered a pillow rest for the heads of those tired with life, has disappeared from the universe. When the human eye looks through the lens of the microscope which investigates the infinitesimal and through the lens of the enormous telescope, which pointed to the heights, reveals the heavens, it has found, above and below, in the atom and in the incommensurable nebula, only one matter, subject to the same laws which have nothing to do with the fate of humans.*

Yet Silva affirms that science, after destroying faith, is itself in no better position to provide guidelines for human life. This negative view of science is evident in "Zoospermos" (*Gotas amargas* 84–86, Sperm). Through the image of renowned German scientist Cornelius van Kerinken, peering through a microscope at spermatazoids, Silva conveys not only the narrow focus of science but also the inherent limitations of humans studying themselves. He reduces science to mere speculation as van Kerinken wildly predicts what the spermatazoids would have become had they been allowed to live. Silva's sarcastic sense of humor emerges when van Kerinken calls the most minute spermatazoid a lyrical poet and the largest a scientist. But underlying such self-deprecation Silva indicates the unfortunate minimization of the professional poet and the aggrandizement of the scientist, which prevails in society to this day:

> el otro, el pequeñísimo,
> algún poeta lírico;
> y el otro, aquél enorme,
> un profesor científico
> que hubiera escrito un libro
> sobre espermatozoides. (85)
>
> *the other one, the smallest,*
> *a lyrical poet;*
> *and the other, that huge one,*
> *a professor of science*
> *who would have written a book*
> *about spermatozoa.*

Van Kerinken goes insane on realizing that science cannot answer eternal questions or truly understand human nature.

Silva reveals his stance that neither faith nor science can explain the meaning and purpose of life in his portrayal of human beings who search hopelessly, without direction, for another truth, faith, or reality to serve as support in the void of existence. "Filosofías" (Philosophy) is Silva's own hopeless negation of everything in life that could possibly give the human being a sense of purpose (*Gotas amargas* 89–91). Through his poetic caricature, "Don Juan de Covadonga, un calavera,/Sin Dios, ni rey, ni ley" (*Libro de versos* 61, Don Juan de Covadonga, a rake,/Without God, without king, without law), he represents the human being's unsuccessful search for religious consolation within the corruption of earthly existence. After leading a life of debauchery Don Juan de Covadonga decides to join his brother Hernando in the convent where he is a prior. However, Hernando quickly disabuses Don Juan of the notion that he will find tranquility, affirming that "todo reviste/Un aspecto satánico, mis horas/Tienen angustias indecibles" (*Libro de versos* 62, everything is sheathed/In a satanic aura, my hours/Have unspeakable anguish). Enjambement supports the intentionally prosaic monotony of Hernando's long description of true convent life. Ascetic confines guarantee nothing, not even a measure of psychic peace.

In his novel Silva further portrays the difficulties and angst that human beings experience in attempting to give meaning to existence. Deeply dissatisfied with his life, his protagonist searches for an external source of guidance only to realize that none exists in a world comprising chance happenings and human fabrications. Fernández declares, "La vida. ¿Quién sabe lo que es? Las religiones no, puesto que la consideran como un paso para otras regiones; la ciencia no, porque apenas investiga las leyes que la rigen sin descubrir su causa ni su objeto" (*De sobremesa* 234, Life. Who knows what it is? Religions do not know, as they consider it a step to other regions; science does not know, because it barely investigates the laws that govern it without discovering its cause nor its object). Fernández reveals his desperate desire for a plan to which he can devote his life. Silva's own depressed sense of worthlessness is audible in Fernández's searing condemnation of what he perceives as his desultory existence:

> Ese obrero que pasa por la calle con su blusa azul lavada por la mujercita cariñosa y que tiene las manos ásperas por el trabajo duro, vale más que tú porque quiere a alguien, y el anarquista que guillotinaron antier porque lanzó una bomba que reventó un

> edificio, vale más que tú porque realizó una idea que se había encarnado en él! Eres un miserable que gasta diez minutos en pulirse las uñas como una cortesana y un inútil hinchado de orgullo monstruoso! ... (*De sobremesa* 250)
>
> *That worker who walks down the street with his blue shirt washed by his loving wife and whose hands are roughened by hard work, is worthier than you because he loves someone, and the anarchist who was guillotined the day before yesterday because he threw a bomb which blew up a building is worthier than you because he turned into action an idea that had taken hold of him! You are a miserable being who spends ten minutes polishing your nails like a courtesan and a good-for-nothing swollen by a monstrous pride!...*

Tragically, none of Fernández's quests to find a guiding norm are wholly successful. He does not find consolation or anything to direct him "por entre las negruras de la vida" (*De sobremesa* 282, through the darkness of life), despite the power and opportunities his wealth gives him to obtain the best medical advice available, to travel as he pleases, to purchase what he wishes, and to associate at leisure with high society. He is ultimately left with an incorrigible sense of emptiness, and consumes his life in worthless dissipation (*De sobremesa* 231).

Like Silva, Castro reveals that neither faith nor science provides a successful means for guiding human beings. Throughout her works she repeats images of the desert and the abyss that convey feelings of emptiness without the support of faith: "¡Que no fondo ben fondo das entrañas/ hai un deserto páramo" (*Follas novas* 281, Down deep inside of one's being/lies a bleak desert). Castro affirms that in the innermost core of the human being lies an abyss that neither laughter nor happiness can fill. Only suffering fills the emptiness. Yet suffering too is baseless for the skeptical human being and leads to self-destruction as only religious faith grants meaning to human pain. When Castro desperately searches for God, all she finds is "la soledad inmensa del vacío" (*Sar* 465, the immense loneliness of nothingness). The loss of faith results in feelings of insecurity: "¿Por que, en fin, Dios meu,/a un tempo me faltan/a terra i o ceu?" (*Follas novas* 300, Why, then, my God,/I lack at the same time/both the earth and the heavens?"). As her religious faith dwindles, Castro recognizes, as does Silva, that science also fails to provide a satisfactory solution for human beings seeking direction. Castro compares the light of a firefly with that generated by a star, concluding that science is unable to answer even basic questions such as the endurance of things in the world:

Una luciérnaga entre el musgo brilla
y un astro en las alturas centellea;
abismo arriba, y en el fondo abismo;
¿qué es al fin lo que acaba y lo que queda?
En vano el pensamiento
indaga y busca en lo insondable, ¡oh ciencia!
Siempre, al llegar al término, ignoramos
qué es al fin lo que acaba y lo que queda. (*Sar* 464)

A firefly shines amid the moss
and a star blinks in the heights;
an abyss above, and an abyss below;
at the last what ends and what remains?
In vain the mind
searches and looks for answers in the unfathomable, oh science!
Always, when we arrive at the finish, we are ignorant
of what ends and what remains.

The imagery in line three can be related to Genesis (1:1) and the darkness of earth and sky before God brought forth light. Castro equates light with a search for spiritual illumination. The light from the firefly and the star contrasts feebly with the darkness of night and relates symbolically to the impotence of human attempts to understand existence. In these lines Castro makes comparisons involving opposites in terms of size, space, depth, and also employs words that imply opposition (*arriba* [above] and *el fondo* [below]; *acaba* [ends] and *queda* [remains]; *indaga* [searches] and *insondable* [unfathomable]) to show the complex, contradictory nature of life. Science, that is, human reason, cannot penetrate beneath or beyond the perplexities of existence to ascertain with certainty if God exists. Addressing doctors, Castro declares that science is incapable of curing or comprehending deeply rooted human suffering:

O meu mal i o meu sofrir
é o meu propio corazón:
¡quitaimo sin compasión!
Despois: ¡faceme vivir! (*Follas novas* 366)

My sickness and my suffering
is my own heart:
wrench it from me without compassion!
Then: make me live!

The alliterating *m* in lines one and two skillfully imitates the sound of human moaning, reinforced by the rhyming of *sofrir* (suffering) and *vivir* (live). For Castro, as for Silva, living and suffering are hopelessly and inexplicably interconnected.

In another poem Castro affirms that in the past, faith guided the hermit to the desert. The hermit symbolizes all humanity who once believed utterly in God. "Desert" for the hermit implicitly signifies the domain of the sun, that is, of heavenly radiance and divine revelation. For Castro it represents a negative landscape in its emptiness as she writes from the perspective of one who has shed blind faith. Like the faithful of former times, she describes how scientists of her day also arrive at the threshold of nothingness. Yet neither the hermit nor the scientist perceives the illusory nature of the reality they have themselves created. Castro concludes that she does not await Ulysses; that is, she does not await a savior in any form but instead affirms that, like Penelope, "tejo y destejo sin cesar mi tela,/pensando que ésta es del destino humano/la incansable tarea" (*Sar* 544, I ravel and unravel my cloth incessantly,/thinking that this is in human life/the unending task). Through this image she emphasizes the radical insufficiency of being human as there is no predetermined design or purpose to life that human beings can discover by faith or science.

Castro writes that, like herself, the new generation is adrift "sin paz, sin rumbo e sin fe" (*Follas novas* 298, without peace, without direction and without faith). She shows how society no longer turns to religion for direction, as faith, particularly among the young, is fading (*Flavio* 317). Churches are empty (*Sar* 465, 516), and the sacred alter is covered with dust (*Sar* 465). Like Silva, Castro maintains that Christian values are no longer socially operative; there is a collective disregard for the emotional and physical well-being of others, including children (*Follas novas* 368–369). Even as she knows society's search will ultimately be fruitless, she reveals the directionless behavior of those seeking a system of beliefs for guidance:

> ¡Aturde la confusa gritería
> que se levanta entre la turba inmensa!
> Ya no saben qué quieren ni qué piden;
> mas embriagados de soberbia, buscan
> un ídolo o una víctima a quien hieran. (*Sar* 502)
>
> *Bewildering is the noisy confusion*
> *that arises from the immense crowd!*
> *They no longer know what they want or what they seek;*
> *but inebriated with pride, they search*
> *for an idol or a victim to injure.*

The expression "ya no" (no longer) indicates that the masses have lost the orientation they once enjoyed. Not sure where to find meaning, a confused society destroys and inflicts pain arbitrarily. In these images Castro thus portrays the lack of transcending purpose in this life, in which suffering, injustice, and confusion prevail. Similarly, Silva believes that lawlessness results from the decline of Catholicism in society. In one poem nihilists "en una súbita explosión/.../Vuelan estatua y orador" (*Gotas amargas* 83, in a sudden explosion/.../burst both the statue and the orator).[17]

In their agonizing conception of human life as radical insufficiency Castro and Silva show how people live without support of any kind. Castro often employs imagery of sickness, depicting pathetically human beings who are infirm and in need of religious sustenance. Adjectives and nouns indicating an absence of health are also frequent in Silva's works reflecting the uncertainty of life and his view of human beings as imperfect, needy, and fragile. Biological orphanhood, symbolic of spiritual orphanhood, is also a thematic constant in Castro's works (*Cantares gallegos* 500, 581; *Follas novas* 272, 282, 293, 309, 316, 354, 369, 407, 425, 432, 438; *Sar* 465, 467, 512, 516). Plaintively she identifies with the moon, "Astro das almas orfas" (*Follas novas* 309, Star of orphaned souls). In *La hija del mar* (Daughter of the Sea) Castro presents a succession of women (Teresa, Esperanza, Candora) who are illegitimate, orphaned, and abandoned. Movingly, Teresa declares that "las caricias maternales son el rocío que da vida a esas pobres plantas que salen al mundo en un día de dolor" (82, maternal caresses are the life-giving dew to those poor plants that come to the world in a day of suffering), thus emphasizing the human need for security. Flavio, Rosa (*Flavio*), and Luis (*El primer loco*) are also orphans who desperately seek meaning in life, which, significantly, they do not find. Likewise, Silva's disoriented novelistic protagonist is an orphan. During his psychoanalysis of José Fernández, Rivington implies that Fernández's desperate groping for spiritual guidance, which has crystallized in an impossible search for the perfect, virginal woman, results from his initial orphanhood (*De sobremesa* 292). He lost his mother and other family members at a tender age. On the death of his grandmother he feels completely forsaken (*De sobremesa* 251).

Conclusion

Unlike Silva, Castro associates herself throughout her writings with humble things and persons. In one poem her speaker is a "diminuto insecto de alas de oro" (*Sar* 533, tiny insect with golden wings) and in another a peasant who has neither food nor firewood in her bare home (*Follas novas* 374–376). As Castro embraces the concerns of humankind, she especially highlights the deprivation that women and children endure through no fault of their own. She is aware that society perceives her as inherently inferior because she is a woman and imposes strict guidelines on her conduct. It was relatively easy for her, therefore, to identify psychologically with the deprived and the lowly, especially considering the circumstances of her birth. Anything she achieved apart from her husband was greeted by surprise and, in the case of her writing, as an outright affront. Silva, on the other hand, affiliates himself mostly with the grandiose, disdaining the mediocrity of society. He imagines living in castles (*Libro de versos* 27) and exalts Bolívar, who possesses "majestad de semidiós" (*Libro de versos* 17, majesty of a demi-god). His constant references to items of luxury also contrast sharply with Castro's imagery, usually taken from nature.

Although Silva's and Castro's response to the limitations of society sometimes differs, both felt restricted by nineteenth-century attitudes. Society expected nothing of Castro because she was a woman and consistently downplayed her literary achievements. Silva, conversely, absorbed his family's and society's high expectations of him as a man, especially with regard to financial security. Silva believed that he had fallen short of these expectations. He was a poet and philosopher at heart, not a businessman. Through his alter ego in *De sobremesa*, a novel filled with wish fulfillment, Silva tragically denounces literary pursuits in favor of materialistic ones. He often uses writing as an unsuccessful attempt to overcome limitations, whereas Castro views writing as a means of exposing injustice wherever she has found it.

Both authors vividly portray experience as negative, with the past denying future endeavors and influencing their general outlook on life. As traditional preconceptions about the meaning and purpose of existence disappear, people remain with nothing but to create a reality based on this experience. Yet Castro and Silva wonder how human beings can create a reality they can tolerate when their experience is only pain and suffering. The two writers convey the deep feelings of emptiness that result from their realization that humans must attempt alone to create their lives in a world permeated by uncertainty. Castro often captures the terrifying force and ubiquity of unforeseen misfortune: "Teño medo á desgracia traidora/que vén, e que nunca se sabe onde vén" (*Follas novas* 279, I am afraid of treacherous misfortune/that comes, and can never be foreseen). Silva similarly writes of the dismaying uncertainty inherent in existence: "Se mezclan a nuestras vidas,/De la ausencia o de la muerte,/Las penas desconocidas" (*Libro de versos* 57, They blend into our lives,/From absence or from death,/unfamiliar suffering). Both often use interrogatives to reveal their metaphysical angst as they question traditional notions about life. Their frequent questioning, irregular rhythms, and use of ellipses display a similar sense of inner chaos, confusion, and fear in the absence of established values. Both are well aware of the anguish resulting from their conception of existence.[18] Their attitude toward life is genuinely and frighteningly speculative. In a church Castro questions in despair, "¿Qué somos? ¿Qué es la muerte?" (*Sar* 464, What are we? What is death?). Similarly, Silva kneels and asks Mother Earth in desperate tones, "¿Qué somos? ¿A do vamos?" (*Gotas amargas* 75, What are we? Where are we going?) He further implores, "Mi angustia sacia y a mi ansiedad contesta" (*Gotas amargas* 75, Sate my anguish and answer my anxiety). For Castro and Silva, suffering has not only very specific outer causes, such as death or poverty, but is also the result of their futile search for enlightenment about human existence. In simple language and sincere voices they transform their suffering into works of art.

Chapter II

The Limitation of Art

As explained in chapter I, the radical insufficiency of being human is the lack of an eternal "human nature" and therefore of a fixed purpose or guiding force in life. Art cannot adequately communicate a conception of reality because subjective perception so deeply affects reality. Castro and Silva emphasize this paradox of artistic creation. Art is merely an expression of the artist's mind, not a means of expressing higher truths.

The shortcomings of art as a means of communication are apparent both in the artist's technical inability to convey her or his vision of life and in readers' misinterpretations. Castro and Silva write about their feelings and thoughts and simultaneously about misgivings concerning their own comprehensibility. Yet even if readers understand, art cannot provide a guidepost that resolves the insufficiency of being human. Moreover, readers may simply repudiate the artists' vision of life.

Castro and Silva acknowledge that uncertainty permeates artistic creation, reception, and perdurability. The question arises as to why Castro and Silva, painfully aware of the possible futility of their endeavor in the realm of art, continue to write.[1] Art allows them to express the problem of human life as deficiency and the resulting fear. Art is an attempt to gain control, to capture meaning through their interpretation of reality by recreating that reality. The uncertainty Castro and Silva experience with regard to the purpose, meaning, and direction of life fills them with such anxiety that they feel inspired to reveal their emotions. Writing becomes an organization of feelings and thoughts, an objective catalog of their innermost concerns. The fearful obscurity they associate with life is evident in the prevailing darkness of their imagery.

Some of Castro's and Silva's most moving verses spring from feelings of *saudade*, the melancholic state of mind born of privations. At times Castro's and Silva's *saudade* has no reference in objective reality "but is a vague and indefinable sense of solitude and loss" (Kulp-Hill 49). For critic Gonzalo Corona Marzol, Castro's *saudade* has no apparent tangible cause but stems from deficiency within Castro herself:

> La saudade de Rosalía tiene su centro en ella misma; es decir, es algo que debería estar en su interior pero que no está. La renuncia, el olvido, o la imposibilidad de llegar a ese algo produce nuevamente la sensación de una presencia caracterizada por su ausencia: el fantasma, la sombra, y el clavo. (50)
>
> *Rosalía's saudade is centered in herself; that is, it is something that should be inside herself but is not. Rejection, neglect, or the impossibility of arriving at that something creates anew the sensation of a presence characterized by its absence: the ghost, the shadow and the nail.*

Castro experiences feelings of orphanhood and insecurity. But perhaps more specifically, another facet of Castro's (and Silva's) *saudade* derives from a deep nostalgia for traditional structures, that is, a yearning to accept life and death within the Catholic tradition, as they once did as children. As adults their keen intelligence, which irrevocably separates them from the majority, allows them to perceive human life as radical insufficiency. Their innocence lost, they feel profoundly different, alone, and afraid. This chapter focuses on thematic and stylistic differences and similarities that substantiate Castro's and Silva's common vision of art as unable to provide a solution to the insufficiencies of life. Critic Kathleen Kulp-Hill's summation of Castro's attitude toward art and creation applies as well to Silva as both attempt to give meaning to subjective existence:

> The words "solitude" and "battle" characterize Rosalía's view of the poet and his art. The poet engages in a lonely and ceaseless struggle to express all of life and to attempt the ineffable. Knowing, with a nod to the scientific enthusiasm of her times, that Science, Progress, and Fame are inevitable, but futile, human pursuits, the poet out of "vice, passion, or, perhaps sickness of soul" continues to cast his bitter drops into the boundless sea. Part of nature that he is, he sings because he must.... Poetry is not written for any self-interested purpose, but arises from the dolorous inner struggle for identity and meaning. (94)

Radical Insufficiency at the Level of the Individual Artist

Castro and Silva: Radical Insufficiency as Catalyst for Creation of Art

The shadow is a recurring motif throughout Castro's and Silva's poetry.[2] It generally represents in both writers the uneasiness they feel about the lack of certainty in life, the absence of guiding principles. Courteau says of Castro, "Critics seeking Rosalía's connections to romanticism have viewed the *sombra* as the expression of a deep, existential *angst*" (1995: 27). Camacho Guizado affirms that Silva's symbolic description of the shadow represents both the past and death (1968: 90). The prevailing image of the shadow in Castro's and Silva's works symbolizes an absence, as of light. But this darkness goes beyond physical conditions. It refers as well to intelligence unable to penetrate the ultimate mystery of existence. As Osiek maintains of Silva, the shadow is "un correlato estético de su punto de vista pesimista" (1968: 22, an aesthetic correlation of his pessimistic point of view). In their best-known poems with shadow imagery, "Cando penso que te fuches" (When I Think That You Have Disappeared) and "Una noche" (One Night), Castro and Silva emphasize the idea of absence. In Castro's case it is a perceived absence of normalcy in a woman compelled to write yet who is viewed as perverse by society. In Silva's, it is the sudden disappearance of a beloved human being, which impels inconsolably to artistic creation.

The "negra sombra" (dark shadow) leitmotif in Castro's "Cando penso que te fuches," (When I Think That You Have Disappeared) so variously interpreted by critics, may actually symbolize the problem of her literary vocation.[3] She clearly feels inhibited from writing because of her gender. Critic Marina Mayoral states, "Tampoco la vocación literaria fue vivida por Rosalía como algo que diese sentido a su vida.... Tenemos la impresión, que se afianzará con los testimonios de *En las orillas del Sar*, de que sus dotes de escritora no las vivió como un don sino como un problema más de su vida" (1993, 2: xvii-xviii, Rosalía did not live her literary vocation as something to give meaning to her life.... We have the impression, later confirmed with the testimonies of *On the Banks of the River Sar*, that she did not enjoy her talent as a writer as a gift but rather as another problem in her life). Tragically, because of the age into which she was born, Castro perceived her need to write as a disturbing inadequacy within herself:

Cando penso que te fuches,
negra sombra que me asombras,
ó pé dos meus cabezales
tornas facéndome mofa.
Cando maxino que es ida,
no mesmo sol te me amostras,
i eres a estrela que brila,
i eres o vento que zoa.
Si cantan, es ti que cantas,
si choran, es ti que choras,
i es o marmurio do rió
i es a noite i es a aurora.
En todo estás e ti es todo,
pra min i en min mesma moras,
nin me abandonarás nunca,
sombra que sempre me asombras. (*Follas novas* 303)

When I think that you have disappeared,
dark shadow who haunts me,
again by my pillow
you return to mock me.
When I imagine your flight,
you appear in the sun itself,
and you are the sun that shines,
and you are the wind that blows.
If they sing, you are the one who sings,
if they weep, you are the one who weeps,
you are the murmur of the river
you are the night and the dawn.
You are in everything you are everything,
for me and in me you dwell,
you will never abandon me,
shadow who ever haunts me.

Her vocation troubles and plagues her. Desperately her poetic voice wishes to flee from the "negra sombra," but whenever she feels she has successfully escaped its influence, it returns, filling her with fear and self-mockery. The epithet *negra* (dark) deepens the blackness of the shadow, emphasizing Castro's negative perception of her vocation, as well as its persistent and negative impact on her life. The emphatic opaqueness of the shadow indicates that Castro does not understand her literary impulse but that she attempts to objectify the shadow and to arrive at some sort of understanding through the act of writing. The paronomastic repetition of *sombra* (shadow) and *asombra* (haunt) in line 2 stresses the enormous effect of the black shadow on her life. The word *asombra* has several meanings. Castro's poetic voice views the black shadow as a looming presence that overwhelms and frightens her. *Asombra* also encloses a more subtle meaning. Castro experiences a sense of awe at the extent and depth of the power of the black shadow within her. When she gazes at the sun, the shadow appears, a negation or darkness that reinforces Castro's opinion of her vocation. The sun is the maximum source of life and energy. The shadow, then, is present, despite her rejection of it, in the most powerful and vital aspects of her existence, in the moments of greatest illumination and, symbolically, in the seeking of higher truths.

Castro subsequently shifts from the presence of the shadow in her life to its designation as the star that shines and the wind that blows. In experiencing the beauty of nature, she is moved to write. When she admires the stars in the darkness or feels the wind, she becomes inspired. Yet persistently underlying such images is her inevitably negative conception of her vocation. On a more literal level a star, consisting of light, is reduced to darkness, the shadow. The wind, associated with creative power in its connection with the creative breath, is often active and violent. In line 9 Castro expresses the idea that wherever people are happy, the black shadow within her sings in chorus. In line 10 she declares that where there is suffering, the black shadow cries too. The black shadow is the murmur of a river, the night, the dawn. Rivers represent fertility, as well as an awareness of the negative flow of time. The black shadow is like the darkness of night and is what darkens the day. On another level Castro reveals that she is inspired to write in response to visual, aural, and tactile sense perceptions that make up the primary imagerial sources of her poetry. The black shadow accompanies Castro everywhere. Her use of anaphora underscores the recurrent apparition of the shadow. Enjambement stresses how the black shadow absorbs her completely, and assonance, less defined than consonance, reflects the elusive presence of the black shadow in her life. The concluding line, a repetition of the second line, becomes a framing within a shadow. Thus through the beautiful and meaningfully ambiguous image of the black shadow, Castro's poetic voice exposes haunted feelings as she realizes that her literary vocation, though problematic, is an integral and mysterious part of her being from which she can never escape.

In *Las literatas* (Women Writers) Castro's persona fervently discourages her friend from literary endeavors, warning that "los hombres miran a las literatas peor que mirarían al diablo" (658, men consider women writers worse than the devil). But even more significant than Castro's awareness of social stigma associated with female writers is her view at times of writing as an abnormal proclivity in women. Novelistic characters Teresa and Mara correlate imagination and confessionary poetry with insanity (*La hija del mar* 82–83; *Flavio* 295). Castro punishes Teresa and Mara, who possess literary tendencies, by making them unhappy, living isolated from mainstream society.[4]

Like Castro, Silva employs the shadow image to underscore the idea of absence. Yet in his case this absence has nothing to do with feelings of inadequacy originating from gender and vocation but rather from inability to sustain possession of a beloved through art. In Silva's poem the shadow represents dark, disturbing, anguished feelings of emptiness in response to the devastating uncertainties of life that overtake and lead him to the creative act itself. His recognition that being human is radical insufficiency induces him, as it has Castro, to seek solace in fantasy. In "Una noche" (*Libro de versos* 32–33) he creates a new realm of existence in which a shadow or soul communes with the shadow of a deceased beloved. With his emphasis on the sacredness and beauty of art Silva views literature as an imperfect, artificial shelter from the imperfections of life. Indeed, the poem stems from the most painful privation of all—the death of a loved one.[5] Polysyndeton and assonant rhyme make the entire poem a prolonged, faltering cry of responsive grief. The poem opens with the brief line "Una noche" (32, One night). The next line begins with the same words, reinforcing the blackness and mystery of night and its association with death, creating through repetition a feeling of uneasy expectancy. Almost devoid of color, the poem is an interlacing of light and dark imagery:

> Y tu sombra
> Fina y lánguida,
> Y mi sombra
> Por los rayos de la luna proyectada
> Sobre las arenas tristes
> De la senda se juntaban ... (*Libro de versos* 32)
>
> *And your shadow*
> *Long and languid,*
> *And my shadow*
> *Projected in the moonbeams*
> *Over the sad sands*
> *Of the path they became one ...*

Black, a privation of light, represents negativeness, hiding. In Silva's poem night and blackness may symbolically refer to a lack of rational understanding of suffering and death. Although white is usually derived from sun symbolism and signifies mental clarity in general, Silva uses light imagery throughout as a means to intensify the darkness of the night and, by extension, the impenetrability of human existence. Fireflies spark "en la sombra" (32, in the shade). Their insignificant light only makes the blackness more intense. Critic Andrés Holguín regards this as "el poema de la ausencia, de la agonía y de la desesperanza en la ausencia. La voz del poeta, sollozante en el segundo canto, golpea en vano contra el infinito negro" (268, the poem of absence, of agony and of desperation in absence. The voice of the poet, sobbing in the second canto, in vain knocks against the infinite darkness). White and black are typically diametrically opposed symbols. White is associated with the positive and black with the negative. Yet here Silva presents white as a noncolor, that is, as lacking in color, and gives it a distinctly negative connotation. In its quality of lividness, white becomes interlinked with death. Silva's poetic voice compares the cold he feels with the cold of his beloved's cheeks, temples, and hands "Entre las blancuras níveas/De las mortüorias sábanas!" (33, Amid the snowy whiteness/Of the shrouds!). Silva's use of epithets when describing the light of the moon actually serves to blanch its color further, muting and reducing it. The moon is "la luna pálida" (33, the pale moon) that shines with "luz blanca" (32, white light). Also the moon, which passively receives its light from the sun, represents in its essence not only death but the mutable as it suffers modifications to its shape resembling the variability of the human condition. The ebb and flow of lines respond to Silva's emotional fervor. Such rhythmic variations create a kinetic effect that imitates the painful changefulness in human life. In the first stanza of the poem there is a noticeable muting of sounds. It is a night "llena de perfumes, de murmullos y de músicas de älas" (32, full of perfumes, of murmurs and the music of wings). The poet's beloved walks beside him "Muda y pálida" (32, Mute and pale). In the second stanza, by contrast, dogs bark and frogs cry out, echoing the poet's agony in the death of his beloved.

The shadow motif that dominates the poem possesses several meanings, all of which connote mystery and emptiness. Shadow refers to darkness: "Una noche/En que ardían en la sombra nupcial y húmeda, las luciérnagas fantásticas" (32, One night/In which the fantastic fireflies glowed in the nuptial and humid blackness). Shadow also means a human silhouette. The shadow, lacking in substance, is the negative double of the body and becomes a general symbolic projection of existential fear in the human being. As the lovers walk down the sandy path filled with foreboding, their shadows are projected by the rays of the moon (32). Silva even uses shadow to refer specifically to death: "Separado de ti misma, por la sombra, por el tiempo y la distancia" (33, Separated from yourself, by the shadow, by time and by distance). In various ways throughout the poem Silva emphasizes the idea of absence. Critic Eduardo Camacho Guizado perspicaciously affirms, "Con la adecuada lectura del poema se echa de ver claramente que al final de casi cada verso existe una pausa, un silencio, unos puntos suspensivos invisibles" (1977: xxvii-xxviii, A careful reading of the poem indicates clearly that at the end of almost every verse there is a pause, a silence, some unwritten ellipses). In response to the death of his beloved, Silva's poetic voice imagines an alternate reality through words in which his soul and the soul of his deceased beloved unite. Yet the bodiless shadow continues to symbolize absence and longing:

> Se acercó y marchó con ella,
> Se acercó y marchó con ella,
> Se acercó y marchó con ella...¡Oh las sombras enlazadas!
> ¡Oh las sombras que se buscan y se juntan en las noches de negruras y de lágrimas!... (*Libro de versos* 33)
>
> *It drew near and left with her,*
> *It drew near and left with her,*
> *It drew near and left with her ... Oh the intertwined shadows!*
> *Oh the shadows that look for each other and come together in the nights of darkness and tears!*

Reflecting his emotional intensity, Silva uses repetition throughout as a mechanism to lend consistency between verses about the past and his present imaginings. But visually these lines become mere shadows themselves. Silva comes to his definition of death as a shadow, a darkness, an emptiness, a negation. It is an absence that fills the living with helpless agony and the writer with an overpowering need to expose the limitations and cruel uncertainties of existence through art.

Castro: Art as a Means of Expression

Art can serve as a vehicle to reveal the anguish and emptiness resulting from the insufficiency of human life. Castro expresses this function of art, claiming in *Follas novas* that sorrow is her muse, a negation with a creative result: "¡Ai!, a tristeza, musa dos nosos tempos, conóceme ben, e de moitos anos atrás; mírame como súa, é outra como eu, non me deixa un momento" (*Follas novas* 269–270, Ah!, sadness, muse of our times, she knows me well, and for many years; she looks upon me as her own and as a like self, does not leave me for a moment). Critic Marina Mayoral affirms that for Castro, "la poesía era un desahogo de los sufrimientos de su vida; escribía, en cierto modo, para liberarse, y por ello se resistía a la publicación" (1974: 296, poetry was an outlet from the suffering of her life; she wrote, in a way, to escape, and because of this she resisted publication). She senses that her verses spring from sickness and absences experienced as powerful privations:

> Mais as cousas teñen de ser como as fan as circunstancias, e se eu non puden nunca fuxir ás miñas tristezas, os meus versos menos. Escritos no deserto de Castilla, pensados e sentidos nas soidades da natureza e do meu corazón, fillos cativos das horas de enfermedade e de ausencias, refrexan quisais con demasiada sinceridade, o estado do meu esprito unhas veces, outras a miña natural disposición (que non en balde son muller) a sentir como propias as penas alleas. (269)[6]
>
> *But things have to be as circumstances dictate, and if I never succeeded in getting away from my sadness, much less my verses. Written in the desert of Castile, thought and felt in the loneliness of nature and of my heart, poor children of the hours of sickness and of absence, they reflect, perhaps too sincerely, at times the state of my mind, at others my natural disposition (not for nothing am I a woman) to make mine the suffering of others.*

However, Castro generally recognizes the failure of art to serve as a satisfactory means of communication. Castro's tone throughout most of her prologue to *Follas novas* is melancholy and pensive. She admits that it has been over ten years since the majority of her poems were written and that her illnesses and the turbulence of her life have not allowed her to reflect on them. Using this admission to excuse the quality of her work, she underscores her persistent artistic insecurity. She refers to her poems as "estes probes enxendros da miña tristura" (*Follas novas* 269, these poor creatures of my sadness). Castro expresses artistic misgivings precisely because of the dark tenor of her writing. She expresses concern that the public may find her plaintive verses tiresome as they cannot understand her subjective perception of life. In collecting poems for *Follas novas* she reveals

> Ó leelos de novo, vin ben craro, como era incompreto e probe este meu traballo poético, canto lle faltaba para ser algo que valla, e

> non un libro máis, sin outro mérito que a perene melancolía que o envolve, e que algúns terán, non sin razón, como fatigosa e monótona. (269)
>
> *Upon reading them anew, I could well understand how poor was my poetic endeavor, how much it lacked to be something of value, and not just another book whose only merit is the constant pessimism that pervades it, and that some may characterize, not without reason, as tiresome and monotonous.*

In a *Sar* poem Castro describes her ultimate determination as an artist, despite public disapproval and rejection of her pessimism, to remain true to the source of her literary inspiration—her own suffering. She reveals, however, that she was once tempted to write insincerely about happy themes in order to please the public and win general acclaim. The public enjoys light, superficial poetry, which is less meaningful and therefore more easily communicated. She affirms that like a god, the poet possesses a thirst for creation, and that thirst is quenched only through genuine inspiration. She concludes that the true substance of art derives from the individual poet's own heart (*Sar* 525). Castro underscores the antithetical literary tastes that exist among the public and the subsequent uncertainty surrounding artistic reception. Precisely because of such uncertainty Castro decides that she will create henceforth indifferent to general opinion. She will use her art to expose, unabashed, her own tragic experience in life and that of the world around her.

In her prologue "Un hombre y una musa" (A Man and a Muse) Castro depicts as a hideous muse her inspiration for *El caballero de las botas azules* (17). Castro's muse is not the popular, universal ideal of a beautiful young girl. Her ugly muse reinforces her novelistic aim of exposing the ugly truth about Madrid society in all its emptiness and falseness through a series of painful confrontations (30, 142–148, 180). Inspired by this unconventional muse, Castro penetrates beneath the surface of human existence at various socioeconomic levels. Her conception of life as radical insufficiency enables her to perceive and, as an artist, to represent the meaninglessness of human beliefs and effort.

Silva: Art as Attempt to Overcome Radical Insufficiency

As with Castro, Silva expresses the notion that writing about somber themes may adversely affect the quality and reception of his writing. However, his concern is not so much that it diminishes the usefulness of art as a means of communication as that it lessens the sanctity of the creative act itself (*Poesías varias* 122). For Silva literature should stand in sharp contrast to the suffering of daily existence. Not surprisingly, he denies the poetic value of his satirical *Gotas amargas* and never seeks to publish them (Litvak 380). He considers lyrical poetry the highest form of art, completely denying the artistic value of satire. At times he evinces discomfort in revealing his innermost thoughts about human suffering, expressing self-reproach when he does so.[7] In early works he represents the purpose of art as a conscious beautification of existence. In his poem "Convenio" (Agreement), the muse, who symbolizes Silva's self-critical voice, declares that she will inspire the poet only if he sings of happy topics: "Descansar quiero ahora de tantas lágrimas;/Hoy he llorado tanto que estoy rendida" (*Poesías varias* 122, I want to rest now from so many tears;/I have cried so much that I am exhausted). The muse protests that humans use poetry egotistically as an outlet for their suffering. She says, though, that she will accompany the poet in writing about the beauty and wonder of nature—an open meadow seen through the branches of trees, the singing wind, and bird nests among the briar—. The muse is very specific in her censure, disclosing her familiarity with the poet's lamentations, affirming Silva's poetic substances as privations:

> Pero tú me prometes no conversarme
> De horrores y de dudas, de rotas liras,
> De tristezas sin causa y de cansancios
> Y de odio a la existencia y hojas marchitas...
> (*Poesías varias* 122)
>
> *But you promise not to talk to me*
> *Of horrors and of doubts, of broken lyres,*
> *Of sadness without cause and of exhaustion*
> *And of hatred of existence and wilted leaves...*

In the poet's verses, lyres, which are symbols of harmony, break, and leaves, typically associated with renewal, fade. Through anaphora and words possessing similar negative overtones, as well as the invariability of the dodecasyllabic rhythm, the muse emphasizes the monotony of the poet's somber repertoire. Likewise, the ellipsis in the final verse implies an interminability to the poet's anguished outpourings. Alliteration, cacophonous in these lines, underscores how the poet's verses contain that which is discordant and unpoetic. Enjambement initially absorbs then depletes the reader. In this poem Silva not only reveals his conception of poetry as something elevated but also shows his conflicting need to express the radical inadequacy of human existence.

In a metaphor derived from Bécquer's Rima V (409) Silva likens poetry to a sacred vessel in which to place whatever beauty one can possibly seize from the insufficiency of life: "Allí verted las flores que en la continua lucha,/Ajó del mundo el frío" (*Libro de versos* 38, Drop there the flowers that in the never-ending struggle,/Were crumpled by the coldness of the world). Silva employs religious imagery throughout "Ars" to emphasize his idea of poetry as something divine. Even the Latin title reinforces his reverent attitude toward art. His tone is meaningfully hushed and pious. The metaphor of poetry as "vaso santo" (*Libro de versos* 38, holy vessel) is especially appropriate because it connotes limitation: within poetry only pure thoughts are distilled from the world. Flowers and pleasant memories are spilled inside the enveloping cup. Flowers symbolize the fragility and transitory nature of life and of happiness. Spikenards, glittering with dew, specifically represent youthful idealism soon extinguished in this world. Silva concludes that poetry, like wine, can intoxicate and serve as a balm to the misery of life. He achieves in his poem a soothing harmony both visual and auditory through a careful selection of images, words, sounds, and a steady rhythm of alexandrines and heptasyllables. Enjambement contributes further to the liquid flow of the poem.

Castro and Silva: Failure to Attain Immortality through Art

One of the central, unanswerable questions of human existence is whether a person's lifeworks are meaningful, perpetuating the memory of the author through them after death. Art is merely an attempt to express an individual's own conception of life, a conception that future generations may not favor or understand. Castro and Silva express misgivings about the durability of the artist's success. They conclude that art, like all human endeavors, is ultimately futile. In an audibly cynical tone, Silva represents with irony the effort that artistic creation implies, only to experience existential "murder" and to become a prisoner to frivolous, changing fashions: "¡Terrible empresa vana!,/pues que tu obra no estará a la moda/de pasado mañana" (*Gotas amargas* 89, Terrible hollow enterprise!/since your work will not be in fashion/the day after tomorrow). Silva recognizes that art as an archetype lies above human attainment. Ideas change from year to year, as do social conventions, tastes, and beliefs.

He thus dispels the hopes of the nonreligious who may have aspired to endure through their art.

Silva also represents the uncertainties of attaining immortality through art in "A Diego Fallon" (*Poesías varias* 108, To Diego Fallon).[8] Movingly, he contrasts the eternal poetry in nature, that is, the objective, with the individual poet, the subjective element whom people forget. Although poets and their art may perish, Silva affirms that artistic sensibility endures in response to the beauty of nature. The forest, where plant life thrives and luxuriates free from any control or cultivation, represents well the unfettered character of poetic inspiration. It is the misty, shadow-filled forest at twilight with its somber cast that most inspires poetic thoughtfulness. The image of the lake additionally displays the possibilities of artistic consciousness and reflection in nature. Trees, which represent growth, proliferation, and regenerative processes, express inexhaustible life and are thus equivalent to symbols of immortality, in implicit contrast to humans and their art. Nests associated with procreation and valleys with fertility reinforce, in the concluding verses, the imaginative fecundity of nature: "Naturaleza amante/Que rima en una misma estrofa inmensa/Los leves nidos y los hondos valles" (*Poesías varias* 108, Loving nature/That rhymes in one immense stanza/The airy nests and the deep valleys). Through anthropomorphization Silva portrays nature as alive and speaking to the visionary. Alliteration reduces words to mere whispers ("selvas seculares" [age-old forests]). Through the muting of sound Silva increases the mystery surrounding poetic nature that prevails over the mortal poet. Assonant rhyme also contributes to the hushed tones of the poem and meaningfully decreases determined outlines, engendering an added sense of vagueness, mystery, and awe.

Castro also represents the transitoriness of writers and their works but in a more matter-of-fact manner than Silva. She affirms that even the great literature of Garcilaso, Calderón, Herrera, Homero, Virgilio "se olvida, no llena ya las exigencias de las descontentadizas criaturas ... no basta a satisfacerlas" (*El caballero de las botas azules* 6–7, is forgotten, no longer fulfills the needs of the disgruntled people ... it is not enough to satisfy them). Castro genuinely never expects or seeks literary fame for herself (*Orillas* 545).[9] Indeed, she wants *Cantares gallegos* (*Galician Songs*) to be published in her husband's name (Kulp 37) as she lives at a time of few women writers in a cultural world governed by old norms of female conduct. In an apostrophe to glory written in indignant alexandrines, she reveals her disparagement of fame, which she feels is often undeserved:

> ¡Cuántos te han alcanzado que no te merecían,
> y cuántos cuyo nombre debiste hacer eterno,
> en brazos del olvido más triste y más profundo
> perdidos para siempre duermen el postrer sueño! (*Sar* 546)
>
> *How many have reached you that did not deserve you,*
> *and how many whose name you should have made eternal,*
> *in the arms of the most profound and sad oblivion*
> *lost forever they rest eternally in slumber!*

In another poem she underscores not only how the living forget the glory attained by the dead but also the democratization that death represents, clearly echoing the medieval theme of *Danza de la muerte* (*Sar* 544–545, Dance of Death). In another she compares glory to a bolt of lightning that amazes for an instant and vanishes just as quickly (*Sar* 545). As a result of her religious doubts, she ponders pessimistically the insignificance of human effort not only in an earthly, but also in a heavenly realm (*Sar* 516).

Because of the uncertainties associated with artistic creation, Castro and Silva conclude that art does not guarantee immortality. For them the passage of time generally impacts negatively on art. Even in the best of cases glory is fleeting and often begins with the artists' own death. Both authors concentrate, therefore, on the disappointing aftermath of personal achievement and the ultimate insignificance of human effort. Castro denies the importance of fame because of injustices and inequities in judging art. Her depiction of art and fame displays a literalness in contrast with Silva's more dreamy conception. Silva's initial idealism gave way to pessimism as a result of disillusioning experiences and realizations. He essentially perceives the purpose of art as a counterbalance, though an unsuccessful one, to the insufficiencies of life. He attempts poignantly to offer quixotic substitutes for the uncertain permanence of art and the artist (*Poesías varias* 116–117). Castro, on the other hand, exposes all aspects of artistic creation to the harsh glare of radical insufficiency without giving illusory, albeit comforting, ways to minimize uncertainty about the continuance of art and the artist.

The Interaction Between Art and Society

Art as Failed Communication

Failure of Society to Understand

Both Castro and Silva recognize that not everyone is capable of apprehending art. Silva writes that half the meaning of a poem, a sculpture, or a painting lies in the work of art itself, and the other half in the head of the reader or contemplator. He is fully aware of the interpretive difficulties that symbolism implies, yet unlike Castro he strives to create comparisons that are imprecise and vague. He realizes that an artist's conception of life cannot be expressed with precision under the best of circumstances. Silva's novelistic alter ego affirms,

> Es que yo no quiero *decir* sino sugerir y para que la sugestión se produzca es preciso que el lector sea un artista. En imaginaciones desprovistas de facultades de ese orden ¿qué efecto producirá la obra de arte? Ninguno. La mitad de ella está en el verso, en la estatua, en el cuadro, la otra en el cerebro del que oye, ve o sueña. Golpea con los dedos esa mesa, es claro que sólo sonarán unos golpes, pásalos por las teclas de marfil y producirán una sinfonía. Y el público es casi siempre mesa y no un piano que vibre como éste… (*De sobremesa* 236–237)
>
> *I do not want to say but rather to suggest and for the suggestion to be effective it is necessary that the reader be an artist. In imaginations lacking that type of talent, what effect would the artistic work create? None. Half of it is in the poetry, in the statue, in the painting, the other half in the mind of the listener, the contemplator, or the dreamer. Drum your fingers on that table, it is true that only some taps will be heard, run them down the ivory keys and they will become a symphony. The public is almost always a table and not a piano that vibrates like this one…*

Even Silva's novelistic character Juan Rovira, who belongs to the cultural elite, significantly confesses that Fernández's diary is unintelligible to him: "Me encanto al oír a los inteligentes recitar tus versos y llamarte gran poeta; de repente se me antoja oírte leer algo como esta noche; pongo toda la atención que Dios me dio, y, mi palabra de honor que me quedo a oscuras de la mayor parte de lo que oigo…" (*De sobremesa* 265, I love to hear intelligent people recite your verses and call you a great poet;

suddenly I wish to hear you read something as you did tonight; I devote all the power of attention that God gave me, and, upon my word I do not understand most of what I hear...).

Silva explores this notion further in "Prólogo al poema intitulado 'Bienaventurados los que lloran' de Rivas Frade" (365–367, Prologue to the Poem "Blessed Are Those Who Weep" by Rivas Frade). He affirms that the brevity of Heine's and Bécquer's verses reflects their conviction of the "inutilidad final del esfuerzo humano" (366, ultimate uselessness of human effort). Silva writes that Heine's irony and mocking laughter are actually a pose to mask his true pain from the bourgeois public, incapable of appreciating the genuine representation of human suffering (367). Eulogizing the deceased poet Luis A. Vergara R., Silva also displays disdain for the public's lack of critical perspicacity in judging and appreciating his poetry. According to Silva, Vergara united childlike innocence and the sobriety of the mature adult, a combination yielding poetical dreams preserved in crystal verses (*Intimidades* 151–153). Crystal, which connotes transparency, suggests that Vergara's delicate poetry can be clearly interpreted and appreciated, yet the public is too insensitive to do so.

In his novel Silva affirms that Hugo, disparaged by society, with its philistine tastes, is fortunate to have died: "Moriste a tiempo, Hugo, padre de la lírica moderna; si hubieras vivido quince años más, habrías oído las carcajadas con que se acompaña la lectura de tus poemas" (321, You died in good time, Hugo, father of modern lyricism; had you lived fifteen more years, you would have heard the guffaws that accompany the reading of your poetry). Silva also disparages the professional critic. He concludes his tribute to Rivas Frade with the following words: "Y si acaso, dentro de algunas semanas los críticos al por menor se ponen a anotarle lunares y a averiguar a quién imitó, yo le contaré a Rivas Frade, para que se ría de ellos" (367, And if by chance, in a few weeks minor critics begin to annotate your work and find out whom you imitated, I shall tell this to Rivas Frade, so that he may laugh at them).

Castro also emphasizes the uncertain nature of artistic interpretation. As critic Marina Mayoral notes, metaphors are scarce in Castro's poetry: "La sustitución de un término real por un término imaginario le produce la inquietud de que su pensamiento no sea comprendido o bien interpretado" (1974: 340, The substitution of a real term for an imaginary one produces an anxiety in her that her thinking may not be understood or may be misinterpreted). In fact, her novel *El caballero de las botas azules*, a truly modern study of the didactic possibilities of literature, underscores the subjective nature of literary interpretation. Intentionally she suspends the reader's traditional expectations in approaching a text: "Los espectadores se devanarán los sesos por comprender su argumento, y te juro que no lo conseguirán" (20, The readers will rack their brains to understand its plot, and I swear to you they will not be able to do so). From the very beginning Castro encourages readers to engage in a close reading of the novel. The unifying element is the duque de la Gloria (*Duke of Glory*), the equivocal protagonist, who aspires to literary fame, as his name implies. He is a fantastic character who possesses supernatural powers and whom Castro superimposes on a realistic nineteenth-century Madrid society. The duke's glorious mission is to orient people so that they will live more productive lives. It is the function of the other novelistic characters to understand both the duke and his enlightened mission. In a literary analogy the duke represents the text to be interpreted and Madrid society his would-be interpreters, successfully applying his message to modify their aimless lives. Alvarez Sanagustín captures the uncertainty of artistic perception through the different ways that each character interprets the duke:

> Cada personaje lo ve o lo intuye desde su peculiar óptica. Un mismo rasgo de su personalidad o de su atuendo es juzgado diversamente, se le atribuyen cualidades contrarias que van del extremo de lo mejor a lo peor, incluso a la síntesis de los contrarios: el bien y el mal simultaneamente. (506)
>
> *Each character sees or intuits him from their particular point of view. A personality trait or aspect of his dress is judged in different ways, conflicting qualities from the best to the worst are attributed to him, even the synthesis of opposites: simultaneously good and bad.*

Yet the majority of the characters in the novel do not penetrate the significance of the duke's redemptive purpose. They concentrate instead, superficially, on his magnificent boots and tie.[10] Castro is satirizing the reader/text relationship and concludes that the didactic value of art is minimal, because of uncertainties inherent in interpretation, including the public's mediocre ability to apprehend art. Castro's intention to question interpretive possibilities of literature becomes clear precisely in the duke's persistent ambiguity. Murguía emphasizes the lack of a determined meaning in the novel: "—¿Qué será? ¿Qué no será?,—se preguntan a cada momento los personajes todos de la obra: no concluye tan mal ésta, cuando el lector al cerrar el libro tiene también que preguntarse: ¿Qué será? ¿Qué no será?" (1944: 154, What is? What is not?—the characters in the work ask themselves constantly: the ending of this one, is not so bad, if the reader upon closing the book has to ask himself: What is? What is not?). In this novel Castro criticizes the bad literature of the age, also revealing lack of confidence in the ability of professional critics to distinguish worthwhile literature from the opposite (40).

Failure of the Artist to Communicate Effectively

Both Silva and Castro conceive of art as an imperfect human creation, as if to confirm Bécquer's definition of poetry as "esa aspiración melancólica y vaga que agita tu espíritu con el deseo de una perfección imposible" (629, that sad and vague desire which moves your spirit with the aspiration of impossible perfection).[11]. Yet although Silva expresses dissatisfaction with his art because it never attains the quality he seeks (Osiek, 1978: 142), he is neither tentative nor insecure about his writing as Castro is at times. Silva's artistic dissatisfaction came later in life when he was near suicide. *De sobremesa* is filled with cutting, self-critical outpourings that emphasize deep feelings of artistic worthlessness:

> No eres nadie, no eres un santo, no eres un bandido, no eres un creador, un artista que fije sus sueños con los colores, con el bronce, con las palabras o con los sonidos; no eres un sabio, no eres un hombre siquiera, eres un muñeco borracho de sangre y de fuerza que se sienta a escribir necedades.... (250)
>
> *You are nobody, you are not a saint, you are not an outlaw, you are not a creator, an artist who splashes his dreams with colors, with bronze, with words or sounds; you are not a wise man, you are not even a man, you are a doll drunk with blood and power who sits down to write inanities....*

The symbolic cancellation of the antithetical groupings of saint/robber and artist/intellectual reinforces the idea of self-negation. Significantly, Fernández dwells most on denying that he is an artist of any kind. Beneath Silva's words lies an intense self-deprecation, loathing, and a sense of inferiority driven by depression and not constituting an accurate portrayal of his opinion of himself as an artist. Silva was displeased not with his literary output but with the public's lack of critical discernment and the inherent inadequacies of language itself. The fact that all Silva's poems have titles and few of Castro's do implies Silva's greater artistic self-esteem. By leaving the majority of her poems untitled, Castro minimizes their individual worth. In addition, Castro blames herself for the public's bewildered response to her verses as she does not adhere to traditional themes and styles. Silva, though, instead deplores the overwhelming mediocrity of society.

Consistently Silva reveals the frustrating limits of words. He would like to render in verse those fragile things that disappear so quickly, such as the pale lily that dies, a moonbeam on a tapestry of moist flowers, and green leaves that open in the warm breezes of May. Yet he finds it impossible to capture the indefinable with words. In the second strophe of "La voz de las cosas," quoted below, his images become even more indeterminate. Implicitly he reveals a desire to accomplish two objectives through writing: he wishes to freeze a reality ever in flux and faithfully to represent emotions and impressions. He realizes, however, that he can accomplish neither. Time passes inexorably and words are an insufficient means of communication. Ghosts symbolize both the numinous and mutable that Silva would like to represent in verse:

> ¡Si aprisionaros pudiera el verso [,]
> Fantasmas grises, cuando pasáis,
> Móviles formas del Universo,
> Sueños confusos, seres que os vais,
> Ósculo triste, suave y perverso
> Que entre las sombras al alma dais,
> Si aprisionaros pudiera el verso [,]
> Fantasmas grises cuando pasáis! (*Libro de versos* 36)
>
> *If only poetry could capture you [,]*
> *As you go by gray ghosts,*
> *Moving forms of the Universe,*
> *Confused dreams, beings that depart,*
> *Soft, sad, and perverse kiss*
> *That in the shadows you give to the soul,*
> *If only poetry could capture you [,]*
> *As you go by gray ghosts!*

Consonance and alliteration in *s* (line 4) emphasize the evasiveness of language as a means of expression. There is throughout a distinct appeal to forward movement, reinforced by such verbs as *pasáis* (go by) and *vais* (depart). All aspects of existence belong to a continuum and cannot be "imprisoned." Lines 1 and 2, repeated at the end, increase the poet's wistful tone. The repetition sets the content in a frame as if to imprison it (in vain). Through carefully selected images Silva relates their ephemeral nature yet meaningfulness, along with the inability of poetry to capture them fully.

He further illustrates the inadequacies of language in "Poesía viva"

(Living Poetry). The poet husband, contemplating his wife who has fallen asleep by the crib of their sleeping infant, discards his own poem of romantic vagaries. Though deeply inspired by the domestic scene before him, he finds that words are insufficient to describe intimate human emotion and "en el labio tembloroso/muere, sin salir, la frase" (*Poesías varias* 112, on the trembling lips/dies, without emerging, the sentence). Like Castro, Silva expresses in particular the limitations of words in conveying feelings but, more often, he wishes to capture emotion of intangible inspiration. In his lyrical prose piece "Suspiros" (Sighs) he negatively contrasts idealized conceptions of life with objective existence. Even happiness realized in human life falls short when measured against happiness imagined in dreams. Echoing Bécquer, he represents the impossible desire to express the ineffable, affirming that words cannot reproduce the sigh born of disillusionment:

> Aun siendo poeta y haciendo el poema maravilloso, no podría hablar de otro suspiro ... del suspiro que viene a todos los pechos humanos cuando comparan la felicidad obtenida, el sabor conocido, el paisaje visto, el amor feliz, con las felicidades que soñaron, que no se realizan jamás, que no ofrece nunca la realidad, y que todos nos forjamos en inútiles ensueños. (361)
>
> *Even as a poet writing wonderful poetry, I could not speak of another sigh ... the sigh that comes to all human hearts when they compare the happiness that is theirs, the taste they know, the scenery they have seen, the happy love, with the happiness we dream, which will never come, which reality never offers, and about which we all dream.*

In "Prólogo al poema intitulado 'Bienaventurados los que lloran' de Federico Rivas Frade," Silva emphasizes the effort exerted by Rivas Frade to achieve universality: "Al fijar alguna impresión fugitiva, por medio de las frases rebeldes, habló para todos los cerebros y para todos los corazones que guardan confusas esas imágenes, sin poderlas reducir a palabras" (365, When setting down some fleeting impression by means of rebellious sentences, he spoke to all minds and to all hearts that keep those vague images unable to put them into words). Published in 1886, "Futuro" (Future), dedicated to Rafael Pombo, is noteworthy considering Silva's youth and his treatment of the increased difficulty that literary creation may presuppose for the aging artist. At one time Pombo's verse, like song, resonated from his innermost being. Yet today the only sounds are those of a chisel as Pombo painfully sculpts a poetry that is unappealing (*Poesías varias* 116). In "Un poema" (A Poem) Silva depicts in graphic terms the essential difficulty in subjugating language at any age: "Y los ritmos indóciles vinieron acercándose,/Juntándose en las sombras, huyéndose y buscándose" (*Libro de versos* 48, And the untamed rhythms came ever closer,/As one in the shadows, fleeing from each other and searching for each other).[12]

In contrast to Silva, Castro reveals self-doubts as a writer. Continually she diminishes the quality of her work, apologizing for her lack of artistry and intelligence (*Cantares gallegos* 487, 490). Critic Claude Poullain writes "Rosalía considera ... que su poesía es un fracaso, y por eso tiene—a veces—la tentación de renunciar. Actitud momentánea, como siempre, pero que muestra hasta qué punto la invade a veces el desaliento" (1974: 179, Rosalía considers ... her poetry a failure, and for that reason she is—sometimes—tempted to stop writing. Momentary feeling, as always, but which illustrates to what point defeat takes hold of her).[13] Her self-criticism stems, in part, from her absorption of negative social attitudes toward female writers and moments of sincere uncertainty about the true value of her talent. But her excessive apologizing is also an appeasement technique to help her survive artistically in a patriarchal society (Stevens 84). She attests that her inspiration for *Cantares gallegos*, Trueba's *Libro de los cantares* (Book of Songs), published eleven years before her own book (Shaw 169), serves as a painful contrast to her own artistic insufficiency.[14] If she possessed Trueba's craftsmanship, she could ennoble the reputation of Galicia in the eyes of the world (*Cantares gallegos* 488). She feels incapable of adequately representing the beauty of her province and the stoic suffering of the Galician women: "As miñas forzas son cativas, quéreas maiores de quen haia de cantarnos con toda a súa verdade e poesía, tan sencilla como dolorosa epopeia" (*Follas novas* 272, Small is my power, more would be required by anyone who would sing to us in all its truth and poetry, such a simple and sad epic). She wishes she could be and do more for Galicia. Sorrowfully she concludes, "Si grasia en cantar non teño/o amor da patria me afoga" (*Cantares gallegos* 634, Although I may lack the wit to sing [its praises]/love for my homeland overwhelms me). As with Silva, Castro was reluctant to publish her works.[15] In Silva's case he hesitated because of his precarious financial position and creditors' views of publications rather than struggling to clear his debts (Osiek, 1978: 32). Also, he disdained the public's inferior artistic acumen. Castro's reluctance was because of the intimate nature of her poetry (Mayoral, 1974: 292) and because of her uncertainty regarding its critical reception as having been authored by a woman, a religious skeptic, and a regionalist. Through an unflattering comparison, Castro communicates just how deeply she repudiated her own writing at times. Her verses, she claims, consist of rocks and ruts. As if written poorly on purpose, they possess the value of a handkerchief. Yet by becoming her own harshest critic she shares in the disdain of patriarchal society, thereby disarming critics and minimizing their disapproval:

> Fas uns versos... ¡ai, que versos!
> Pois cal eles non vin outros,
> todos empedregullados,
> e de cotomelos todos,
> parecen feitos adrede
> para lerse a sopramocos. (*Follas novas* 368)
>
> *You write poetry ... ah, what poetry!*
> *I have never seen the like,*
> *stony, rutted,*
> *with ups and downs and debris,*
> *they seem to be composed*
> *to be read as a handkerchief.*

Castro truly believed that women, possessing acute sensitivity, were ideally suited for lyrical poetry (*Flavio* 296). Throughout her life she opposed negative preconceptions about female writing, yet she had to confront her own psychological insecurities because of those preconceptions and to function within the confines of patriarchal society.

In Castro's opinion artists' failure to use art effectively stems both from technical incompetence and also, as in Silva, from the intrinsic deficiencies of the artistic medium. Castro affirms "*La palabra y la idea* ... Hay un abismo/entre ambas cosas, orador sublime" (*Sar* 534, Word and thought ... An abyss/separates both things, sublime orator). In one of her most powerful poems, "¡Silencio!" (*Follas novas* 286, Silence!), Castro confirms the passion she feels as an artist, as well as her doubts about her artistic ability and the sufficiency of words to convey thought and emotion. Her dream of attaining immortality through art comes into direct conflict with these feelings of artistic inadequacy and the limitations of words themselves. The dramatic opening of "¡Silencio!" may represent either the emptiness of words or Castro's angry command to herself as an artist. Written as a silva, with a single strophe, the poem seems to flow in a torrent, like artistic inspiration. She contrasts the image of excitedly dipping a pen into her swollen vein with the hand that moves clumsily across paper. Through these images she exposes the artist's difficult task of externalizing passion through the highly mechanical process of writing. Ellipses in line 12 convey both the arduous task of creation and its empty results: "escribo ... escribo ... ¿para que?" (*Follas novas* 286, I write

... I write ... for what?). By extensively modifying nouns, Castro graphically represents how the artist struggles to define and shape thought, remaining eternally discontented. She compares what she would like to express with what she actually can. The artist will always experience feelings of insufficiency when comparing the completeness and beauty of what is in the heart with mere words. Castro orders the tempestuous images of fervent artistic inspiration, born in the dark regions of her inner being, to return to their source where other such images have died, unable to live satisfactorily on paper. She concludes her poem, therefore, by contrasting the purity and definition of the artist's inspiration and its representation, now veiled in the darkness of the artist's own deficiency and of the inherent inadequacies of language: "¿Da idea a forma inmaculada e pura/donde quedou velada?" (*Follas novas* 286, The form of the idea clean and pure/where was it lost?)

In particular, Castro expresses the frustrating limitations of words to capture intimate emotions, but, as opposed to Silva, she is concerned about adequately reproducing more familiar emotions, such as love and hate. In a *Sar* poem that emphasizes auditory imagery she affirms that the artist can reproduce singing birds, kisses, leaves rustling in the wind, stormy seas, the crash of thunder but cannot adequately describe the sound of a breaking heart. Such a heart beats in silence that no artistic talent can render successfully in words. At best the poet can create similes. The heart that beats without love is a sound so sad, so tragic, "que jamás el genio pudo/repetirlo con sus ecos" (*Sar* 520, that genius could never/repeat it with its echoes). Language is the convergence of the outer and inner worlds. Yet in another poem Castro similarly reveals the powerlessness of words to impart deep emotion. Human beings moved by profound hate or love stammer helplessly because "la lengua humana, torpe, no traduce/el velado misterio" (*Sar* 535, the clumsy human tongue, cannot reveal/the shrouded mystery).

Radical Insufficiency at the Level of Society

Contemplation of Art: Failed Attempt to Overcome Radical Insufficiency

Even if art could effectively communicate the artist's intent, the contemplation of art cannot overcome the radical insufficiency of being human. In fact, Silva and Castro reveal that contemplation of art cannot even provide a temporary balm to heal the basic inadequacy of life. This is a conclusion Silva came to late in life. Art is merely a continuance of the human being, not something higher. Critic C. M. Bowra accurately affirms that in "Avant-Propos," the opening poem of *Gotas amargas*, Silva represents the idea that "la ficción no es suficiente y que la verdad se impone de manera inexorable" (78, fiction is not enough and that truth will impose itself inexorably). Silva explores this notion further in his novel *De sobremesa*. His novelistic protagonist José Fernández searches anxiously and fruitlessly for an artistic ideal that he can contemplate and that can lend meaning to his existence. Fernández embodies this artistic ideal in the unnaturally pale and beautiful Helena Scilly Dancourt (*De sobremesa* 320). Orjuela affirms, "La Helena de *De sobremesa* es ... una abstracción que representa el ideal de perfección inalcanzable y el paradigma del arte prerrafaelita" (1990: 433–434, Helena in *After-Dinner Chat* is ... an abstraction representing the unattainable ideal of perfection and the paradigm of Preraphaelite art). In this last desperate book, written only weeks before his suicide, a depressed and hopeless Silva depicts through Fernández's search for Helena that art is a subjective and unenduring representation of life and thus cannot provide guidance or meaning for human existence. Wrongly, Fernández believes that his amorous ideal will afford him psychological, emotional, and spiritual support. Dr. Rivington, to whom Fernández appeals for spiritual and physical direction, owns a portrait that looks astonishingly like the elusive Helena. But the painting is actually of Helena's dead mother. According to Charvet, another doctor, the portrait is not even a faithful representation of Helena's mother, as art cannot truly reflect life: "El amanerado imitador de los prerrafaelistas no hizo más que dañar el modelo al sujetarlo a las invenciones de su escuela, porque la muerta era más hermosa todavía" (314, The affected imitator of the Preraphaelites did no more than harm the model by subjecting it to the inventions of his school, because the dead woman was more beautiful still). Dr. Rivington gives a copy of his portrait of Helena's mother to Fernández as a present. But it soon becomes clear that neither Fernández's own poetry nor his contemplation of paintings make him feel any less disillusioned or influence his life in any positive way.

Silva also shows that the artist in Fernández seeks impossible perfection through Helena in terms of beauty and purity. That he finds Helena dead gives the lie to the idealistic notion that perfection exists in any realm of life other than dreams. Emphasizing Helena's symbolic meaning as a vision that appears out of the inscrutable darkness of his existence, Fernández asserts, at her graveside, "Tal vez no hayas existido nunca y seas sólo un sueño luminoso de mi espíritu" (*De sobremesa* 350, Perhaps you have never existed and you are only a luminous figment of my mind). Fernández sadly resolves, "Voy a pedirle a vulgares ocupaciones mercantiles y al empleo incesante de mi actividad material lo que no me darían ni el amor ni el arte, el secreto para soportar la vida" (*De sobremesa* 348–349, I shall ask of common business tasks and never-ending toil what neither love nor art would give me, the secret to endure life). Fernández's declaration is a self-surrender to mere matter, a kind of existential suicide or capitulation to what exasperated the idealistic Silva. Therefore, Fernández expresses his disillusionment with the idea that the contemplation of art (writings, paintings) can elevate him to a plane higher than physical existence.

Castro, for her part, questions the purpose of artistic creation, which she believes replicates what others have done before:

E ben, ¿para que escribo?
E ben, porque así semos,
relox que repetimos
eternamente o mesmo. (*Follas novas* 277)

And so why do I write?
And so, we always go
as the clock that advances
eternally the same.

The heptasyllabic verses of the poem reinforce the idea of sameness. Anaphora in lines 1 and 2 also emphasizes lack of change. The image of the clock strengthens her point about the mechanization and dehumanization of the writer. The clock also stresses the circular questioning of writers like Castro, who search endlessly for nonexistent answers and solutions to life. The stylistic monotony relates not only to the lack of anything substantive to say, but also, as in Silva, to the basic emptiness and unfulfilling nature of art. Words lacking in connotative value increase the intentionally monotonous tone of the poem. Although both authors use art as an attempt to clarify their ideas or express attitudes about life, on contemplating their own works and those of others they sadly realize that art cannot make existence meaningful or provide guidance as there are no universal truths or messages to be conveyed.

Failure of Society to Accept Art

Even if art could be communicated effectively and understood, society may simply reject the artist's vision.[16] As seen in the life and works of Castro and Silva, social conventions and traditions form major barriers to society's acceptance of art.[17] Certainly, Castro provides ample testimony of social pressures resulting from her vocation and gender.[18] Critics of her time feel threatened by her successful use of the vernacular to convey themes of universal human concern, as well as by her inquiry into metaphysics.[19] They classify and dismiss her as a minor provincial poet to silence her political, social, and religious heterodoxy (Pardo Bazán 683).[20] Castro herself notes that her poetry is innovative in form and rhythm: "as imaxes de múltiples formas,/de estranas feituras, de cores incertos" (*Follas novas* 277, images with multiple forms,/of strange compositions, and uncertain rhythms). Such innovations serve too as an obstacle to critical acceptance of her work. Dedicating most of the *Sar* prologue to recounting critical injustices, Murguía asserts that "la crítica de entonces le echó en cara, como una gran falta, la de adoptar metros inusitados y combinaciones nuevas" (1993: 449, criticism of Castro's day accused her of grievous fault, of adopting uncommon rhythms and new combinations). Castro is aware that increased subjectivity poses problems in understanding art. Yet these unusual forms spontaneously surface as a reflection of her inner state of confusion about existence.

Both writers' productions give tangible expression to the breaking away from established literary norms and, symbolically, from preconceptions of the way things should be. Silva also conveys that his innovations have not met with critical acclaim.[21] In "Un poema" he describes his disillusioning experience in creating a poem of extraordinary rhythms, as he breaks ground for new ways of attempted communication. The poem does not have a single period in the nineteen lines preceding the last, heightening the reader's anticipation and making the ending all the more dramatic: "Le mostré mi poema a un crítico estupendo.../Y lo leyó seis veces y me dijo ... No entiendo!" (*Libro de versos* 49, "I showed my poem to a great critic.../And he read it six times and said ... I do not understand!.[22] Silva writes his poem in couplets. He represents through the number two his desire to achieve harmony and artistic balance through creative achievement. The concluding couplet structurally reinforces Silva's repeated assertion that the creative process necessarily involves both artist and critic and that these two may be, as in this case, in direct conflict. His entire poem consists of showing the arduous nature of artistic creation only to have his "obra audaz y suprema" (*Libro de versos* 48, "audacious and supreme work") dissolve with the critic's laconic "No entiendo!" (*Libro de versos* 49, I do not understand!), which ends the work in a brusquely ironic manner. It is the critic, not the poet, who appears utterly ridiculous.

In their times, Castro's and Silva's literature received mixed critical reviews, thereby representing the uncertain fate of art. Mayoral accurately observes that "es un tópico decir de algunos autores que han sido maltratados o ignorados por la crítica. En el caso de Rosalía responde a la más estricta realidad" (1976: 44, it is a cliché to say about some authors that they have been mistreated or ignored by critics. In Rosalía's case it is nothing short of the absolute truth). In Silva's case critics supporting the prevailing conservative morality during his life prevented a fair judgment of his artistry and depth by suppressing or deforming his works and image to support their conservative agenda (Mejía 473).

Conclusion

Castro and Silva admit eternal dissatisfaction with language as a means of artistic expression and with the critical reception of art. They continue to write, however, because they feel compelled by the shadow, that is, the expression of their anxiety in response to the uncertainty of life. But just as art cannot provide certainty or the comfort of immortality to the artist, neither can it provide society with a means for overcoming radical insufficiency. Art is only itself a projection of the deficient human being. Moreover, there is never an unlimited time period to accomplish goals. Neither Castro nor Silva truly enjoys the fruits of the writer's labor or fulfills all the writer's cherished literary dreams. Yet what they do write is both eloquent and meaningful as they attempt to understand human existence. During Castro's life, though, her gender, dialect, and metaphysical depth served as impediments to the acceptance of her work. Unlike Castro, Silva experiences no shame attached to his literary vocation. However, his cynicism and suicide prevented his full acceptance as an artist. These authors fully acknowledge the ephemeral, uncertain nature of fame. In *La hija del mar* (153–154) and in "Un hombre y una musa" (*El caballero de las botas azules* 3, A Man and a Muse) Castro disdains posthumous glory for happiness in life. Murguía affirms repeatedly that Castro possessed no desire for literary glory (1944: 145). Castro's negative attitude toward fame is conditioned to a great degree by society's condemnation of female artistic ambition. Silva's disparagement of renown stems from his disdain of critical and popular assessments of art. In the manner of Fray Luis de León, Silva extols the joys of rustic simplicity as superior to glory (*Intimidades* 140–141). He also reassures Rafael Pombo in "Futuro" that although he and his verses may not be remembered, his memory remains in all that is truly poetic, "como entre las negruras del vacío/La lumbre sideral de las estrellas" (*Poesías varias* 117, as amid the darkness of a vacuum/The sidereal fire of the stars). Thus, the silent beauty of Pombo's inspiration shines forever forth like starlight in the empty darkness. Both Silva and Castro are too genuine as artists ever to have sacrificed artistic integrity for public and critical acclaim.

Chapter III

THE UNCERTAINTY OF LOVE

Castro and Silva lived in societies that believed in romantic love as an ideal and lasting union that spiritually elevated men and women. Romantic love, which viewed love as a perfect completion to human life (Singer, 2: xi), possessed specific traits as a sentimental tradition. First, romantic love often involved a desire to achieve a permanent and stable union with a member of the opposite sex (Singer, 2: 299). Second, this form of loving discerned a value intrinsic in love itself, whether or not the amorous ideal was worthy of that love (Singer, 2: 299). For the romantic, love requires no self-justification (Singer, 3: 20). Another aspect of romantic love implied that sexual love between men and women was in itself an ideal worth seeking (Singer, 2: 300). Last, romantic love professed the belief that love allowed people to experience life more fully and deeply, permitting them to learn truths about the world that only passion, not reason, could unlock about the nature of reality (Singer, 2: 286). Indeed, romantics perceived the very act of loving as divine. Those who adhered to this tradition thought that its godliness resulted from the ability of love to unify, purify, and redeem human nature (Singer, 2: 294).

Yet Castro and Silva show that their characters are incapable of having a love that lasts because (1) death intervenes; (2) outside circumstances intrude on their lives; or (3) they lack the depth to sustain such an emotion. These themes constantly recur, underscoring the fact that Castro and Silva did not view such frustrations as isolated instances. Instead, the overall impression is that these obstacles are inevitable in every relationship, and, consequently, lasting love is impossible.

In her exploration of this idea Castro proclaims her belief in the existence of genuine, often crippling, emotion. This is particularly evident when she treats the emotional pain caused by the death of a loved one and when she describes the suffering of lovers separated because of Galician emigration. In one poem Castro's poetic voice tenderly personifies thoughts and memories of her husband, a Galician emigré. Enjambement underscores the urgency of her plea for his return as does repetition in line one:

> ¡Volve, volve onda min, porque anque diga
> que consolada vivo
> con estos loucos pensamentos, seica,
> seica me axudan a morrer, Dios mío!
> (*Follas novas* 429)
>
> *Come back, come back to me, although I may say*
> *that I am consoled*
> *by these crazy thoughts, they only,*
> *perhaps help me to die, my God!*

Deprived of her husband's company, Castro reveals her acute loneliness through the fantasies of her poetic voice. Because the circumstances of human existence are constantly in flux, love often remains unfulfilled. Silva's approach is more intellectual and cynical. Many of his characters are incapable of true emotion. The others attempt to perpetuate love through mere fantasy. Whereas Castro focuses on the impact of changing circumstances on love, Silva treats romantic love as an irrational denial of change. He maintains that love is an illusion attainable only by shutting out the world and thereby imposing a fictional stability on personal experience. For instance, in "Una noche" his poetic voice describes the intermingling of his shadow with the shadow of his dead beloved: "(Oh las sombras que se buscan y se juntan en las noches de negruras y de lágrimas!..." (*Libro de versos* 33, Oh the shadows that search for each other and come together in the nights of darkness and tears!...) In "Realidad" (Reality) Silva's poetic voice contrasts dreams of idyllic love that he and his beloved share with harsh existence (*Intimidades* 148–150). Hence Castro and Silva show that love is fraught with the same uncertainty that pervades all human existence.

Through their representations of false, frivolous, and unrequited love, Castro and Silva also refute the romantic idealization of love as inherently worthy in itself. They express the pain associated with superficial and unreciprocated love, emphasizing lingering, negative psychological effects that lead to a loveless, meaningless life. Castro and Silva repeatedly refer as well to the unfulfilling nature of carnal love, which they reduce to mere biological impulses. With sadness, they depict characters who erroneously believe that commitment to human relationships can fulfill their longing for security and completion in the radical insufficiency of human life. These authors emphasize too that neither conjugal nor spiritual love provides a source of stability and permanence.

Although their contemporaries impose idealized notions on love, making it seem lasting, perfect, meaningful, and fulfilling, Castro and Silva penetrate beneath conventional attitudes to see love as something imperfect, fleeting, and conducive to great sorrow. For them the search for perfect love is an impossible quest for absolutes and ideals. The two authors describe the pain that results from the attempt to harmonize idealistic conceptions of love with workaday life. Castro views romantic love as distinctly misleading. Silva also recognizes the split between the everyday and the ideal but tends to highlight the dependence of romantic love on imagination. Both writers present characters whose excessive idealism leads to love not of an actual person but rather of their own dream of love as they fantasize about that person. Few of their characters find or keep a meaningful relationship. Outer factors separate those who love, and even when in a relationship, Castro's and Silva's characters feel separated, disjointed, incomplete, and unfulfilled.

These fictional experiences therefore reveal the deficiencies of the concept of romantic love. Castro and Silva indicate that love arises out of a person's unique experiences, emotions, and intellect. For the two authors love is not an objective moral force but a feeling that each individual synthesizes from intimate thoughts and circumstances. They find that love cannot give guidance and meaning to an individual because the feeling of love originates with the individual. In other words, love cannot relieve people of responsibility for their own lives and, consequently, cannot overcome radical insufficiency. Because Castro and Silva adopt this individualistic and empirical view of love, romantic love is to them a great falsifier (*Follas novas* 419–420; *Intimidades* 175–177). In their worlds, people cannot look to love to give meaning to life. Instead, because human beings create love, they must provide meaning for themselves.

However, Castro and Silva present this theme in different ways (*Sar* 527; *Gotas amargas* 76–77). For Castro the promise of romantic love remains unfulfilled. Her characters feel an emotion that, in its intensity, may approach the feelings described by romantic love. But these emotions are fleeting and get washed away by harsh experience. In one poem her speaker bitterly reveals, through her own tragic life story, her beloved's empty promises of eternal fidelity (*Follas novas* 419–420). Castro contrasts the events of her characters' lives with social conventions and in this way reveals the superficiality and absurdity of society's belief in romantic love (*Flavio*

463). She consequently fills her writings with detailed studies of the life experiences and emotions of her characters. By reflecting on everyday living, she concludes that love is an outgrowth of experience, and because circumstances are constantly changing, fulfilling love cannot endure.

Yet Castro clearly shows anxiety about losing the false comfort of romantic love. As a result, her writings bridge the traditional notion of romantic love and a new conception of love as a reflection of radical insufficiency. Just as Castro herself feels the tension between romantic love and actual experience, so do her characters. Unable to reconcile the two, they feel deep dissatisfaction and frustration. Their failure to create any meaning for themselves to fill the gap left by romantic love frequently leads to their destruction (*Ruinas* 727 [Ruins]; *El primer loco* 758). Unlike Silva, Castro does not idealize men or women in her writings. Her characters are capable of love and deception, these individuals may be attractive or otherwise, and their relationships may display not only tenderness but also bitter complaints. In one brief poem Castro's speaker angrily determines to neglect the rosebushes and pigeon house of her emigrated beloved just as he has neglected her: "que sequen, como eu me seco,/que morran, como eu me morro" (*Follas novas* 417, let them dry up, as I dry up,/let them die, as I die).

As in Castro, in Silva love not only stays unfulfilled but is also unfulfillable. He often denies the depth of true emotion and portrays the concepts of love and of spiritual union between two people as artificial and pathetic. For Silva the world derives its vulgarity from the early frustration of his high expectations. He begins his career with greater idealism than does Castro. Hence, the discrepancy between his idealism and his actual experience is much starker and more startling. According to critic C. M. Bowra, in later poems "Silva abandona sus caros ideales románticos y simbolistas, y se burla de ellos considerándolos ilusos. La vida no es así en modo alguno, piensa, sino mucho más deprimente y abyecta" (77, Silva abandons his cherished romantic and symbolist ideals, and mocks them thinking them illusory. Life is not like this at all, he thinks, but much more abject and depressing). Looking to writers Rivas Frade, Bécquer, Heine, José Angel Porras, and Emilio Antonio Escobar, Silva affirms how their romantic idealizations of women "se han desvanecido al ponerse en contacto con la realidad" (366, have disappeared on coming in contact with reality). Silva's novelistic character Monteverde perspicaciously asserts of José Fernández, Silva's alter ego, that in response to his surroundings, "tú vas soñando siempre con alguna Dulcinea" (*De sobremesa* 346, you are always dreaming about some Dulcinea).

For Silva love is a mere fantasy, and he dramatizes this point by describing love in terms of symbols and dreams. He perceives the crudeness of the everyday world but does not immerse himself in it as does Castro. For him the archetype of love is unattainable, whereas Castro deals more with the perception of women from within and therefore is more in tune with the practical experience of the human limits of love. Clearly, though, both authors deeply distrust traditional notions of romantic love. Yet once they strip away its veneer, they have little left to which they can cling. The unsuccessful struggle to fill the resulting gap shapes their artistic productions.

The Fictionality of Romantic Love

Failure Because of the Instability of Life

Death

Castro and Silva show that even when people share feelings of oneness through mutual love, this love may end tragically because of the unexpected intervention of death. The resulting emptiness often causes the surviving lover to acknowledge futiley the depth of his or her passion, as well as to feel incomplete and disoriented. For both Castro and Silva, the inevitability of death represents the most emphatic denial of the possibility of lasting love. Castro suggests that the death of a loved one may, in fact, preclude the ability to love ever again. She sadly maintains, as does Silva, that the past limits the capacity to love in a meaningful way. In particular, negative experiences influence future actions and outlook. In one poem, reminiscent of the medieval romance "Fonte frida," Castro expresses the pain of human life as radical insufficiency as a young widow grieves the loss of her beloved husband. She is unwilling to accept a new lover, as happiness and hope for her have died forever:

> Que a rula que viudou,
> xurou de non ser casada,
> nin pousar en ramo verde
> nin beber da iaugua crara. (*Cantares gallegos* 594)[1]
>
> *The widowed turtle dove,*
> *swore never to marry again,*
> *nor to alight on a green bough*
> *nor drink the clear water.*

Castro describes how another woman whose beloved has passed away wishes only to die. In utter despair she unsuccessfully attempts suicide by drowning (*Follas novas* 433).

Silva insists more than Castro on the theme that lasting love can only exist in an imaginary world where death is nowhere to be found. He often pathetically expresses the impotence of the strongest human love when confronted by death (*De sobremesa* 313). In "Poeta, di paso" (Poet, Say Softly) the rays of the moon do not penetrate the dense jungle foilage, symbolically implying the initial conviction of his poetic voice that death cannot touch him and his beloved in their ecstasy. The physical consummation of their love is in itself a celebration of life. By the end of the first stanza, however, the moon appears amid the night mist, its silvery beams filtering through the branches to suggest the subtle, ubiquitous presence of death in human life. At the young woman's funeral the flickering mortuary candles are tragically reminiscent of her trembling in sexual rapture. Her lover's shock and despair reverberate in his final exclamation: "Y estaba helada y cárdena tu boca que fue mía!" (*Libro de versos* 29, And your lips once mine were now icy and purple!)

Similarly, in "Una noche" Silva describes the anguish death brings another young lover. Initially, the interconnected shadows of lover and beloved form one long shadow, graphically representing the intactness of their love. However, with the death of one of the lovers, the survivor expresses his privation of happiness in life. As he walks down the same path, only one shadow remains, and he cries out in desperation and loneliness,

> Y mi sombra
> Por los rayos de la luna proyectada,
> Iba sola,
> Iba sola
> ¡Iba sola por la estepa solitaria! (*Libro de versos* 33)
>
> *And my shadow*
> *Projected by the rays of the moon,*
> *Walked alone,*
> *Walked alone*
> *Through the lonely steppe!*

The fact that at the end of the poem the unified shadows represent mere fantasy underscores Silva's pessimism about the attainability of lasting love.

Work Obligations

Castro also portrays how the demands of life can impede the ability to achieve enduring happiness in love. She reveals this theme most dramatically in her writings on the emigration of men from Galicia in which work needs and geography separate those who love, causing great sadness. For example, in "Adios, ríos; adios, fontes" (Good-bye, Rivers; Good-bye, Fountains) an impoverished Galician leaves home and his beloved to seek his fortune elsewhere, anticipating the possibility that he may be forgotten (*Cantares gallegos* 543). Another Galician emigré compares the promise he and his beloved made never to separate, with delicate rose petals dispersed by cold winds, symbolic of what actually has taken place (*Cantares gallegos* 577). A sorrow-stricken woman pleads with a river on its way to the sea to take her tears to her beloved, who has emigrated to Brazil. The steady octosyllabic rhythm may well suggest the woman's constancy, the flowing river the theme of loss and oblivion through its representation of the passage of time: "Pasa, pasa, caladiño,/co teu manso rebulir,/camiño do mar salado" (*Cantares gallegos* 555, Quietly, quietly go along,/gently bubbling,/on your way to the briny sea). In a similar poem the narrator appeals eloquently to a swallow that crossed the ocean with her mate, now missing, to depart again and bring her news of his whereabouts. Through repetition Castro stresses the wife's keen loneliness and despair, and asyndeton hints the relentless monotony of her life without her husband's loving presence:

> Tecín soia a miña tea,
> sembrei soia o meu nabal,
> soia vou por leña ó monte,
> soia a vexo arder no lar. (*Follas novas* 414)
>
> *Alone I wove my cloth,*
> *alone I sowed my turnips,*
> *alone I gather firewood in the mountain,*
> *alone I burn it in the hearth.*

The images of weaving, planting, and a fire blazing in the hearth all relate to home and the impulse of life, in stark contrast to the woman's feelings of disorientation and emptiness. These poems depict the suffering of Galician women who must live alone as "viudas de vivos e mortos" (*Follas novas* 407, widows of the living and the dead) while their men attempt to find work in other regions. Bitterly Castro reviles Castile, to which so many Galicians emigrate, only to die, leaving loved ones to grieve

(*Cantares gallegos* 598–599). Castro also pessimistically notes how forced emigration may become a means for men to engage in extramarital affairs far from disapproving eyes, and she thereby indicates the superficial nature of their love. One emigré refuses to return home to his wife, explaining that although "Antona está alá, teño aquí a Rosa" (*Follas novas* 427, Antona is there, Rosa is here). As Kulp states, "Galicia is identified with the poet on a feminine level, as a woman abandoned by her men" (218). Castro believes that to live alone and forgotten is the worst kind of suffering (*Follas novas* 367), whereas Silva deals much less with practical problems and does not dwell on how the exigencies of life separate those who love.

Failure Because of Imperfect Love

False or Frivolous Love

Romantics believed in love for the sake of love and maintained the perfection of love in itself (Singer, 3: 19). However, for Castro and Silva love is most often a deluded state, especially in its initial stages. Love begins for Castro as a dizzying flight of heavenly surprises that inevitably become "inaplacable angustia,/hondo dolor del alma" (*Sar* 538, inconsolable anguish,/deep pain of the soul). Through her novelistic character Mara she expresses her most personal conception of love as "una llama brillante que ardía algunos momentos y se apagaba después para siempre" (*Flavio* 387, a brilliant flame that burned for a few moments and went out forever). Silva similarly describes the wondrous beginnings of love that always fade, like flowers once belonging to the beloved (*Intimidades* 209). Both writers express how intellectualizations of the amorous ideal or of the concept of love often lack substance because they do not reflect objective existence. A contrast emerges, however, in their depiction of love as delusion. Castro reveals keen suffering when a lover fails to perceive the beloved with accuracy and is only living under an illusion that the beloved possesses attractive qualities. Many times Castro gives the union of opposites as a reason for failed love. Silva, on the other hand, tends to counterpose preconceptions about romantic love with vulgar everyday experience.

Most of Castro's poems and novels treating the theme of love describe the anguish and despair people experience as they come to acknowledge the unpleasant truth about their relationships. In a poem lighthearted in essence Castro nevertheless presents a charming bagpipe player, who turns out to be a flashy but false lover, deceiving young village girls. Arriving in different towns, this musical Don Juan complacently sings at break of day, "*Con esta miña gaitiña/ás nenas hei de engañar*" (*Cantares gallegos* 522, With my bagpipe/I shall fool the maidens). Indifferent to their feelings, he seduces the innocent girls, whom Castro compares to fragile butterflies, while she envisions the bagpiper as the light that burns them. In "Vivir para ver" (Live to See) María recounts how a faithless beloved entreated her to wait for him, insisting that only death could keep him from returning to her side. Remaining true to her promise of future love, only as an old woman does María realize the tragic repercussions of her constancy (*Follas novas* 420). Castro indicates that women in particular tend to misjudge the emotional capacity of their suitors. In "N'é de morte" (Nobody Dies), for instance, Rosa endows her beloved with a sensitivity he does not possess, and she unconsciously exaggerates his love for her until he indifferently shatters her dream of romantic love (*Follas novas* 420–421).

Yet not all Castro's false or inconstant lovers are men. Many are women (*Cantares gallegos* 528). Her novelistic character Montenegro loves a young woman whose superficiality only becomes apparent to him later (*Ruinas*). However, in *El primer loco* Castro emphasizes that Luis' love for Berenice is a product of his imagination and persistent self-deception. In this way Castro represents the propensity of lovers to idealize the beloved, which inevitably leads to suffering.

Repeatedly, Castro expresses sincere concern over the transience and superficiality of human love:

> Son los corazones de algunas criaturas
> como los caminos muy transitados,
> donde las pisadas de los que ahora llegan,
> borran las pisadas de los que pasaron:
> no será posible que dejéis en ellos,
> de vuestro cariño, recuerdo ni rastro. (*Sar* 527)
>
> *Some hearts are*
> *like well-worn paths,*
> *where the footsteps of the newly arrived,*
> *erase the footsteps of those gone by:*
> *it will not be possible to leave in them,*
> *any remembrance or trace of your love.*

Developing her simile in lines 1 and 2 she gives the impression of continuous movement, like the love that so swiftly enters and leaves frivolous hearts. Her prosaicism reflects the weariness and disappointment she feels. Pessimistically she affirms that love, like all that is sweet in life, "canto máis come un del, repuna logo" (*Follas novas* 325, the more you taste it, it sickens you). Yet Castro is not bitter about the ephemerality of love. Rather, she is sentimental and longs for the time when she believed that love was permanent.

Silva is more cynical about love than Castro. To drive home his attitude toward ephemeral love, he shows no interest in character portrayal as such. In "Luz de luna" (Moonlight) he invents a fictional Jezebel. The poetic voice displays shock and dismay at the woman's superficiality and the brevity of human love (*Libro de versos* 56). Indeed, the poem "Día de difuntos" (Day of the Dead) questions the capacity of human beings to sustain meaningful love of any kind, romantic or familial (*Libro de versos* 64–68). In the ironically titled "Idilio" (Idyll), which may refer to Silva's initially innocent conception of love, a second speaker, the voice of experience, mercilessly strips away romantic illusions, emphasizing the tenuous nature of human love (*Gotas amargas* 92). Silva does not comment on the harsh content of the poem but makes his satire of romantic love more effective through direct dialogue. Repeatedly, both writers depict the bright expectations that the experience of love inevitably dashes.

Unrequited Love

Humans' quest for love may also fail if they unwittingly fall in love with someone who cannot or will not return their love. Romantics idealized the pain involved in love by making it self-validating (Singer, 3: 30). Indeed, they believed that the worthiest kind of love was that which remained unfulfilled (Osiek, 1978: 126). Castro and Silva, however, do not concur. They find such love pointless and empty. Insisting that fulfilling love requires reciprocity, they also recognize that because love implies interdependency, there is no way to be sure of another person's subjective response and particular situation in life. By focusing on these one-sided "relationships" Castro and Silva conclude that love is a creation of each individual, rather than the romantics' enduring spiritual union between two individuals, able to offer personal fulfillment and orientation.

Castro frequently portrays painfully intense unrequited loves. She starts with the simple notion that two people in the same circumstances may perceive those circumstances differently. She presents this theme in a dialogic poem in which a woman unequivocally proclaims that she will remain faithful to an absent lover, duplicitous and cruel: "—Anque me odie, e me pise, e me maldiza,/heillo de perdoar" (*Follas novas* 416, Although he may hate me, mistreat me, and curse me,/I shall forgive him). The poetic subject in another poem declares her desire to give the lover the purest scent if she were a rose, the gentlest murmur if an ocean wave, the most loving kiss if the dawn's light, but then, sadly affirms, "si Dios ... máis ben sei que ti/non qués de min, nin a groria" (*Follas novas* 422, if God ... I well know that you/would not even want heaven from me). The relationship is not in any way spiritually fulfilling.

In another poem Castro describes the frustration of a country girl whose love is not reciprocated:

> Máis ansias teño, máis sinto,
> ¡rematada!,
> que non me queira Jacinto,
> nin solteira, nin casada. (*Cantares gallegos* 524)
>
> *I feel it and it exasperates me,*
> *wretched one!,*
> *that Jacinto does not want me,*
> *neither single, nor married.*

The speaker here reveals through repeated negation that she clearly understands her loveless predicament: she knows her zeal cannot make up for her beloved's indifference. Castro conveys the force of privation, that is, the lack of fulfillment the girl experiences and how it actually intensifies her passion. The Galician writer often portrays characters who are captives of love, unable to break psychologically from a beloved who causes them endless suffering. Indeed Castro shows at times that unrequited love may actually serve as a stimulant to love as lovers hope that their own passion will penetrate the beloved's indifference, as in Esmeralda's relationship with Luis in *El primer loco*. Yet Castro eloquently underscores the tragic emptiness of such love (*El primer loco* 739). Thus, she shows that love is not a higher spiritual union between two people but a feeling that grows out of each person's unique personality.

Whereas Castro focuses on the emotional pain caused by unrequited love, Silva concentrates on the power of unrequited love to give rise to fantasies to dull the distress produced by the realization that romantic love cannot exist. In one poem Silva's speaker reveals to an absent, unresponsive beloved that he still dreams "en tu amor y en tu belleza" (*Intimidades* 165, in your love and your beauty).[2] In "Sub-umbra," whose title suggests secrecy, Silva describes how imagination takes over in answer to unrequited love. The poem is one long, excited sentence, like a secret whispered into the ear of the beloved. Anaphora bestows a sense of insistent urgency on the words of his poetic voice as he explains how he has overcome his beloved's neglect through dreams: "Aunque me olvides, aunque no me ames/Aunque me odies, sueño contigo!" (*Intimidades* 131, Though you may forget me, though you may not love me/Though you may hate me, I dream about you!) Yet his love stays unfulfilled because he has only empty fantasies to hold. The utter devotion of Silva's poetic voice toward his beloved vividly recalls the similar fidelity of Castro's speaker in her previously mentioned poem, *Follas novas* (416). In both cases the lovers continue to care despite the rejection of the beloved. In another poem by Silva an unrealized dream of love causes Silva's poetic voice to yearn for the release of death (*Intimidades* 130). Both Silva and Castro portray impossible love not as a nobler kind of love but as something inadequate and irrational.

Carnal Love

Romantics viewed passionate love as a symbol of the special oneness achieved between male and female. Human sexual relationships acquired inherent goodness through idealization of the sexual experience (Singer, 2: 301; 3: 11). Romantic love elevated sexuality into something transcendental rather than something simply biological (Singer, 3: 19). Castro and Silva, however, undervalue physical love and emphasize the disenchantment that results from treating sexual relationships as episodes in a series.[3] These writers often equate love to mere libidinal impulses (*Flavio* 461; *De sobremesa* 324). They reveal little constancy in love and indirectly indicate the decline of Catholic values in society as unmarried men and women engage in sexual affairs and married people in adulterous liaisons without fear of condemning their souls. Silva and Castro repeatedly show that indiscriminate passionate love is not a purifying or elevating experience but rather a completely unfulfilling one.

Silva's protagonist José Fernández is caught up in a world of unbridled promiscuity.[4] Cynically, he reflects on the corruption of society, "en que el adulterio es fácil y practicable, como un *sport*" (*De sobremesa* 336–337, in which adultery is easy and feasible, like a sport). However, despite his numerous affairs, he finds carnal love unsatisfying, leading to boredom and self-loathing. He experiences only feelings of emptiness and confusion rather than a solution to the radical inadequacy of life. In "Egalité" Silva reduces sexual union to a meaningless, primitively instinctive physical response between a man and woman. Equating king and commoner through their sexuality, Silva deflates the preconception of copulation as a more significant and reverent act at higher social levels (*Gotas amargas* 93). In "Lentes ajenos" (Borrowed Spectacles) he emphasizes not only the artificiality of human love in general but also the lack of emotional nurturing that carnal love provides (*Gotas amargas* 76–77). He describes in another poem how a young man's libido brings him to a prostitute with whom he does not experience the ecstasy that romantic love promises (*Gotas amargas* 80). Castro also condemns a society filled with sexual promiscuity for its moral degradation and the dissatisfaction to which it leads.[5] In one poem nocturnal mist represents an obscuring of moral outlines. Margarita, a virgin, becomes lost in both a literal and figurative sense when she seeks and finds passionate love (*Sar* 470). In Margarita's ultimate unhappiness Castro stresses the unfulfilling consequences of carnal love.

Having rejected romantic love, neither author finds a satisfying solution to the radical insufficiency of human life and its resulting emptiness. They see the world in terms of the conflict between actual experience and romantic love. Once they have determined that romantic love is a false ideal, their worldview leaves them with only one alternative—awareness of bitterness. Sadly, they accept the fact that life is nothing more than experience and instinct.

Conjugal Love

Another romantic idealization often establishes love as a lasting union through marriage (Singer, 2: 299). Castro and Silva, however, reject the notion that conjugal love enriches life and endures. These writers depict loveless spouses as pitiable and tragic. Silva's novelistic characters stay in empty marriages not because of ethical principles but rather out of convenience or simply out of acceptance of the façade of marriage as a social institution.

Castro and Silva repeatedly describe married life as unenviable. Ultimately joined merely by legal and ecclesiastical bonds, partners come to feel alienated and unsatisfied. For these writers the ideal of marriage falters under everyday, mundane existence. Both authors agree that marriage attempts to perpetuate what may be a fleeting emotion. Spouses come to the painful realization that the stability which marriage purports to create actually may undercut the vibrancy of life and the evolution or development of the individual through experience. People cannot overcome their changing personas and achieve permanent "oneness" with one another. Castro and Silva show the impossibility of stasis in human relationships. As critic Rosalinda Schwartz affirms, "la orientación total de Silva se cimenta en este principio del dinamismo cósmico, del cual la historia sentimental humana forma parte" (374, Silva's total orientation is based upon this principle of cosmic dynamics, a part of which is the human sentimental history). Both authors recognize that change is the very essence of life.

Silva and Castro present marriage, the symbol of the durability of human love, in pessimistic terms. For example, in Silva's poem "Nupcial" (Nuptial) a young woman gets married with great anticipation. For her the ringing church bells echo with future happiness. Despite her hopeful dreams and the convivial atmosphere of the wedding celebration, the poem concludes on a solemn note as violin strings throb with the melancholy of a dying day, foreshadowing only sadness (*Libro de versos* 43). Silva visually divides the thematically similar poem "Sus dos mesas" (Her Two Tables) into two strophes with the titles "*De soltera*" (As a Single Woman) and "*De casada*" (As a Married Woman), highlighting the differences between these two states. When single, the woman has on her table symbols of dreamy grandeur typically associated with love: flasks with engravings containing diaphanous scents, a rare and fragile vase with flowers, precious stones in a red silk case, and a love letter. After marriage, the woman's table exhibits prosaic objects: a baby's bottle, scissors, spoons, and a diaper (*Poesías varias* 109). Silva thus contrasts the dreams of love and marriage with ensuing disillusionment.

For Castro marriage consists of "Celicios, cantos poder;/penitencias, a Dios dar" (*Follas novas* 364, Cilicia, by the pound;/penitences, without end). Although many see her as the quintessential pessimist, her pessimism is less corrosive than Silva's. Like him she debunks marriage, but she injects some humor as her poetic voice declares that she will marry in winter as "¡non ter quen lle a un quente os pés!..." (*Follas novas* 365, one must keep one's feet warm!...). Frequently she incorporates pointed yet humorous diatribes about marriage (*Follas novas* 395–398). Beneath the humor, though, lies the tragic reality of a loveless existence. Although Castro agrees with Silva that it is usually women who suffer in marriage, she can conceive the opposite case: Xan suffers the martyrdom of a marriage to Pepa, a lazy shrew: "mentras seu home traballa,/ela lava os pés no rego" (*Follas novas* 387, while her husband toils,/she painstakingly washes her feet). In a poem light in tone yet tragic at base, Castro portrays the economic reality of marriage for poor women. In pleading to Saint Anthony for a man, an impoverished young woman exclaims: "*dádeme un home,/anque me mate,/anque me esfole*" (*Cantares gallegos* 536, give me a man already,/although it may kill me,/or he may kill me). In the past, economic, political, and other impersonal considerations controlled marriage. Yet both authors also affirm that marriage based on emotional foundations is equally precarious.

Spiritual Love

In the radical insufficiency of human life Silva and Castro show how humans may turn to the amorous ideal for more than just a passionate relationship; they may seek a spiritual oneship. They hope that the beloved will somehow be able to help them set their lives on a meaningful and fulfilling course. Romantics idealized the strength of love, believing it capable of turning sinners into saints (Singer, 3: 16). This idealization generally stems from the belief in the all-transforming power of love when two people unite rather than in any positive qualities the lovers may possess in themselves. Romantics essentially believed that love itself was magical (Singer, 3: 19). Proponents of romantic love also maintained that true love consisted of an ideal relationship that was not observable in empirical form. They believed that love between two people allowed them to reach greater heights, to participate in the divine (Singer, 2: 285). Castro and Silva, however, reject the romantic notion that love can elevate an individual to a higher spiritual plane. For them, it is meaningless to speak of love as anything but a product of human emotions and consciousness. Silva and Castro believe that love cannot lead to spiritual fulfillment. It cannot elevate an individual above the limits of personal emotions and experiences because it is an outgrowth of those emotions and experiences.[6]

Silva illustrates this theme in his novel *De sobremesa*. His protagonist, José Fernández, dissatisfied with life, associates fifteen-year-old Helena, his amorous ideal, with spiritual salvation (Orjuela, 1976: 29).[7] After seeing this child-woman only twice, he attributes to her supernatural powers, believing that she will guide his poor, sick soul (*De sobremesa* 272). Helena, an ethereal being, remains so throughout the novel, and Fernández does not succeed in finding support and sanctuary through her love.

Although he engages in carnal love, Fernández repeatedly appeals in vain to Helena to save him by declaring that carnal love is unfulfilling: "Estoy harto de la lujuria y quiero el amor; estoy cansado de la carne y quiero el espíritu" (*De sobremesa* 295, I am tired of lust and I want love; I am tired of the flesh and I want the spirit). He seeks a pure and perfect love comprising higher ideals, not merely sexual need. Desperately he struggles against his sexual impulses that subjugate his idealistic aspirations for Helena. However, his libido overwhelms him. Throughout his quest for Helena's pure love, he repeatedly succumbs to other women (*De sobremesa* 333).

Silva shows that spiritual love does not lead to moral betterment. In fact, Fernández's disillusioning experiences in love alienate him further from God, increasing his anger and aimlessness. After he unexpectedly discovers Helena's grave, his amorous ideal can never disillusion him now; neither can she provide the answers and guidance he had sought. Through his shrine to Helena, Fernández despondently worships the elusive dream of perfect love and the spiritual regeneration that she embodied.

De sobremesa brings into relief the dichotomy between the concept of romantic love, represented by Fernández's perception of Helena, and actual experience, seen in his sordid love affairs. He believes in romantic love, but this belief cannot overcome his natural urges. He struggles with the impossible task of reconciling his carnal love with his love for Helena. He sees the extremes of impossible idealism and base lust. Yet he receives no spiritual gratification from his feelings for Helena and no fulfillment from his cavorting with prostitutes.

Like Silva, Castro depicts the quest for spiritual love. In her novel *El primer loco* Berenice is the amorous ideal of the protagonist Luis. Like Fernández, Luis believes that his beloved is an expression of divinity. He insists that human language is too plebeian for Berenice, "aquella criatura semi-divina" (687, that girl almost divine), thus exemplifying his exaggerated concept of her. Yet Luis' imaginative perception of her is more real to him than the woman of flesh and blood herself. In fact, his friend Pedro sees her as a very ordinary, even vulgar woman. Whereas Silva's Fernández never interacts verbally with Helena, Castro's Luis does with Berenice. Luis persistently idealizes Berenice and their relationship in order to make both conform to his conception of perfect love. As with Silva's Helena, Castro's Berenice represents an unsuccessful search for absolutes, reflecting the metaphysical anxiety of both authors. Luis in essence creates Berenice (685). Like Silva's Helena, Berenice is pure idealization. Luis does not accept Berenice as merely the reality she is herself but as a romanticized version of that reality. The refusal or inability to see the beloved as she truly is results in Luis' blind affirmation of love as perfect, enduring, and uplifting. But Luis' love for Berenice does not cause her to love him, nor does it elevate him. Indeed he has shamefully abused Esmeralda verbally as the symbol of his temptation to violate his love for Berenice. Luis confesses that Esmeralda physically resembled Berenice and for that reason "enconaba mis heridas tornándome duro, extravagante y brutal con ella" (733, festered my wounds making me hard, extravagant and brutal with her).

Neither Castro's Luis nor Silva's Fernández reaches any higher truth or knowledge through his experiences with love. Both authors show, though, how human beings desperately yearn to believe in something greater than themselves. They recognize that in the radical insufficiency of human life people poignantly and unsuccessfully seek through love the same stability, support, and guidance that religion once provided.

The Disillusionment of Love

Castro and Silva emphasize that romantic love perpetuates unrealistic expectations that leave lovers feeling thoroughly disenchanted. Both authors show that disillusionment is inevitable for those gullible enough to begin life with the hope that romantic love is possible. In Castro's and Silva's writings no satisfying alternative exists to romantic love, and such a dearth increases feelings of disillusionment. Characters must choose between the idealized morality of romantic love and the unfulfilling and directionless pursuit of base desires. Castro and Silva depict love as a painful experience, with loneliness as its dénouement. For Silva as for Castro the ultimately unhappy outcome of love always intrudes, negating even memories of joyous moments shared with the beloved (*Intimidades* 210–211; *Follas novas* 304). Silva views the passage of time as negative because of its unfavorable impact on the conservation of love. Castro considers the passage of time both in negative and positive terms. Time adversely affects the sustainment of love, yet time also heals the rawest wounds of love, leaving the lover forever numbed by disillusionment. Both authors reveal how time erodes personal romantic beliefs about the meaning and permanence of love.

Practically nonexistent in Silva's and Castro's works is pure love, which would give meaning and direction to life. When it does appear, as between the lovers in "Una noche" (*Libro de versos* 32–33) or between Esperanza and Fausto (*La hija del mar*), it inevitably dies. Indeed, Silva bases the premise of his entire novel on a lack of innocent, redemptive love as Fernández searches unsuccessfully for the chaste Helena. Silva also underscores the absence of innocent love in society through his poem "Perdida" (Lost), in which a man impregnates a trusting young woman then deserts her (*Intimidades* 163–164).[8] In the novel *La hija del mar* Castro likewise depicts a lack of virtuous love through pirate Alberto Ansot's incestuous love for Esperanza, his biological daughter.[9] Castro also represents through her novelistic character Mara (*Flavio*), an unsuccessful search for innocent love. Mara's skepticism about love, which contrasts with Flavio's initial idealism, is the product of her greater worldliness. Critic Kathleen Kulp-Hill comments that for Mara, "idealism and perfect love, incarnated by Flavio, are disappointed. The price of his love is enslavement, annihilation of identity and will, which she cannot accept" (126). Mara retreats from all social interaction, becoming a recluse, because she never wants to feel vulnerable to the pain of love again. Like Silva's Fernández (*De sobremesa After-Dinner Chat*), she can only conceive of pure love as a fond but impossible dream.

Both Castro and Silva suggest that their disillusionment with love stems from observed and from lived experience. With sadness they point out the prevalence of materialistic attitudes associated with love. They emphasize that materialism in love is negative because it causes people to overlook moral, intellectual, and personal qualities. Luxury both fascinates and blinds Castro's protagonist Flavio. Eventually he rejects Mara, young but of modest means, for an older yet wealthier woman (289). In *Ruinas* Montenegro's poverty incapacitates him for integrating into society despite the nobility of his character (679). Cynically, Silva's novelistic protagonist also confirms the prevalence of materialistic love among people of fashion (333).

Castro and Silva are pessimistic about the possibility of finding happiness and fulfillment in love. Critics underscore the insistent disillusionment these authors associate with love (Mayoral, 1974: 133; Osiek, 1978: 59). Both are similar in their resignation to suffering. All their characters become passive sufferers in love, acknowledging frustration and disappointment as inevitable. Silva insists on early disillusionment against the suffering that love inevitably yields, advising the cauterization of sentimental wounds (*Gotas amargas* 81). Castro, too, sensitively affirms that she writes about the sadness love brings because "un cauterio es el que yo quiero aplicar a ese pobre cuanto rebelde corazón" (*El primer loco* 711, I want to cauterize this suffering but rebellious heart).

Conclusion

Realizing that romantic love is an illusion, Castro and Silva face a dilemma. Accepting the concept of romantic love is intellectually dishonest and inevitably disappointing because romantic love and actual experience are irreconcilable. Rejecting this concept, however, results in a psychological vacuum, leaving the individual directionless and isolated. But Castro and Silva do not avoid the painful confrontation between love and life. Instead, they underscore the anxiety produced by the possibility of loss through death, abandonment, or rejection. Silva's characters most often respond by seeking solace in illusion, whereas Castro's isolate themselves by rejecting future relationships. Both authors demonstrate that by idealizing love and believing in its permanence, lovers fail to account for the uncertainty and harshness of existence. They also reveal that lovers suffer more when they possess idealistic expectations about love. Both insist, too, that suffering because of love does not make people stronger and more noble but rather more cynical and sad.

With deep regret these authors emphasize the precarious nature of love because they realize that love cannot satisfy basic human needs for direction, purpose, and meaning. Castro expresses the uncertain outcome of love: "Dos seres pueden llegar a amarse; pero no siempre la suerte les señala un mismo camino ni la misma fuerza los atrae" (*Flavio* 374, Two people may come to love each other; but fate does not always point them in the same direction nor do they experience the same force of attraction). Silva too highlights the unpredictability of human emotion. Wistfully his poetic voice contrasts painted butterflies on a fragile urn with a woman's eyes that sparkle each morning with fickle desire (*Libro de versos* 42). In the search for stability and meaning Castro and Silva often portray characters for whom love has become an obsession to fill the emptiness of life. Yet they show that love is a failed attempt to overcome the radical insufficiency of human life. Neither mutual, unrequited, carnal, conjugal, nor spiritual love brings happiness, fulfillment, or purpose to life but, instead, only confusion, pain, and sorrow.

Chapter IV

Death as Limit and Possibility

Castro and Silva grew up in the Catholic tradition, which brooks no ambiguity about the existence of God. In this scheme the circumstances and events of a person's life form part of a divine plan. The acknowledgment that a divine plan exists provides spiritual comfort and grants meaning to life and death. The faithful perceive innocent suffering as lying beyond human comprehension, as a product of God's will that He rewards with eternal happiness in the afterlife. However, Castro and Silva are critical of Catholicism, which they cannot accept blindly in their view of human existence as radical insufficiency. Intellectually and emotionally they find it difficult to reconcile tragic life experiences with the divine plan of a merciful God. They persistently reveal doubts about whether God or an afterlife actually exists. The possibility that God may be merely a delusion fills their writing with terror and anxiety as they struggle to find meaning in life, especially in reference to human suffering. Moreover, death becomes frightening in the uncertainty of what lies beyond. The two authors show that the inevitability of death and the incertitude of the Afterworld create enormous pressure to accomplish goals, leading to an acute awareness of the passage of time. Both repeatedly express how time constrains human life. However, although Castro and Silva display a sense of urgency when they depict the passage of time, they also pessimistically indicate how people often live anxiously without a defined purpose (*Follas novas* 363–364; *De sobremesa* 231). Uncertain about the presence of a divine plan and feeling the pressure of time, Castro and Silva at times adopt a carpe diem mentality. With the belief that existence may have no purpose, these authors urge mere pleasure seeking. However, they reveal that this outlook proves ultimately unfulfilling. Consequently,

Castro and Silva become desperate. They see inescapable suffering as the lot of humans and express uncertainty about its greater significance. As a result, they come to embrace the only certain fact of existence: that death ends suffering on earth. They therefore frequently view death as a desirable and sensible option, despite the uncertainty of the hereafter. The themes of death and spiritual crisis that permeate their writings inextricably refer to the facts of their lives. The logic of their thought is clear enough, but it is the surrounding circumstances of their lives that make the emotional content of their writing understandable.

Castro and Silva grievously acknowledge their spiritual crises. Although Castro loses her faith, she struggles valiantly to regain it. She longs for the comfort of Catholic beliefs, however doubtful she may have found them, and would, if she could, live an unquestioning life. Confronted by suffering and failing to rekindle her faith, however, she yearns for the numbness of death. Silva, on the other hand, accepts the nonexistence of God as an unavoidable though deeply troubling fact. Unlike Castro, he does not try to recapture a faith that has slipped away.

The Uncertainty of God and an Afterlife

The two authors' religious dilemma arises from the fact that they yearn to understand the world logically. Their failure to correlate suffering with an all-powerful, benevolent God causes them to doubt God's existence and the possibility of an afterlife. Once they have challenged God and His divine plan, however, they are left without direction. Indeed, the road and journey symbolism that abounds in their works (*Flavio*; *De sobremesa*) emphasizes a lack of direction in life. Castro and Silva thus understand that people are in a condition of radical insufficiency, without external guiding principles. As Kulp suggests, Castro depicts the radical inadequacy of life in a way similar to Unamuno, that is, as "man's ability to think, to suffer, to be conscious of himself as a unique individual, and his inability to know his fate or to find the absolute" (156–157). This is an unnerving conclusion for Castro and Silva, raised to believe in a universe filled with divine meaning. Thus, throughout their writing, these authors express a sense of anguish and personal drama: their intellect causes them to doubt God's existence, yet their human condition compels them to seek God's comforting presence. Both writers reveal feelings of loss as they reject their Catholic beliefs, once an integral part of their identities (*Sar* 465; *Intimidades* 147). Although they never recover their religious faith before their deaths, a contrast emerges in the evolution of their thoughts. In Castro's later works, especially *Sar*, there appear occasional flashes of hope that perhaps God and the afterlife exist. Silva, on the other hand, grows increasingly pessimistic about the existence of God and the possibility of an afterlife, with deep cynicism as the hallmark of his later works.

Castro understands and sympathizes with those who believe in God, given that such faith can comfort (*Sar* 465). In fact, she herself deeply wants to believe. She argues that those who die trusting in God, even if deluded, are truly fortunate, "No importa que los sueños sean mentira" (*Sar* 466, It does not matter that dreams are lies). Yet she cannot accept spiritual comfort at the expense of truth. Therefore, she needs God to prove His existence. In a dialogue she poignantly speaks to God about her religious crisis and records in painstaking and intimate detail her unsuccessful battle to believe in Him because of what she sees as the arbitrary nature of human suffering (*Follas novas* 332). The dialogistic format of poems treating her problematic faith symbolizes her painful lack of spiritual integration (*Follas novas* 315–316).[1] Constant misfortune, which she likens to an ever-hungry she-wolf, erodes her faith (*Follas novas* 332–333). At the root of Castro's crisis of faith is human suffering, which she cannot accept or comprehend. She also finds Catholic dogma troublesome; it is hard for her to approve eternal suffering in hell "cuando el pecado es obra de un instante" (*Sar* 540, when the sin lasts but one instant).

However, Castro is at times contradictory in her religious struggle, revealing the poignant anguish of her search for God. As Mayoral affirms, "Unas veces se le imponía una visión de la vida absurda y sin sentido; otras, el deseo de encontrar un sentido a la existencia le hacía volver a las antiguas creencias" (1974: 60, Sometimes she held an absurd and meaningless view of life; at others, the desire to find meaning to life caused her to revert to her old beliefs). Castro implores God to restore the religious faith she had when she was young: "Vuelve a mis ojos la celeste venda/de la fe bienhechora que he perdido" (*Sar* 465, Return to my eyes the blessed blindfold/of the soothing faith that I have lost).[2] Mayoral interprets Castro's yearning for "la celeste venda" (the blessed blindfold) as a contradiction of the disbelief Castro voices in her other writings (*R. de Castro* 104). The metaphor of the blindfold is a paradox that Castro purposely cultivates to depict the pitiful human state. The blindfold represents the human being's frightening loss of blind religious faith and pathetic efforts to restore childhood illusions against the disorienting glare of fuller consciousness in adulthood. She acknowledges the innocent religious convictions of the young and longs as an adult for similar ignorance, despite recognizing the delusional nature of such faith. In maturity she portrays religious belief as the negation of light or truth about the nonexistence of God. Therefore, the blindfold symbolizes human denial about the lack of meaning and purpose for suffering and death in the radical insufficiency of human life. In this poem, as in others, Castro represents the psychological benefits of human dreams (*Sar* 519). She recognizes that faith protects human beings from the keenest suffering, as it lends comfort and coherence to life and earthly torment. Castro wishes to believe in God wholeheartedly as she once did as a child so that she may find relief from an existence that is miserable and completely incomprehensible. She realizes that life can only be truly meaningful within the context of faith. As she scrutinizes the mystery of the natural world, the beauty of art, her fear of death, and her feelings of aimless drifting on earth (*Sar* 464, 471–472, 514–518, 521, 526), her poetic voice turns to Jesus Christ, with whose suffering she identifies, affirming that she anxiously searches for God "como el piloto en la tormenta busca/la luz del faro que le guíe al puerto" (*Sar* 553, as the pilot in the storm seeks/the ray of the lighthouse to guide him to port). Though her search is full of painful doubts because of her uncompromising honesty, she continues with her religious struggle, because she longs to accept God's existence.

Ultimately, however, she cannot completely dispel her doubts and acknowledges the abandonment of the human being in the world. She sees no positive evidence of natural revelation. Winds that disband clouds merely reflect disorder (*Follas novas* 290). In one poem Castro implies that when humans gaze up to heaven, they see only marble statues of angels that they themselves have created (*Sar* 465–466). She cannot overcome her uncertainty and conveys the power and insidiousness of doubt (*Sar* 473). For her "en mil pedazos roto/mi Dios cayó al abismo" (*Sar* 465, broken in a thousand pieces/my God fell to the abyss). Her image of a shattered God may represent her unsuccessful attempts to support God's existence through reason. In another poem she describes a somber blackness that lies at the core of her being, representing a lack of religious illumination or faith, and the pessimism it engenders (*Follas novas* 305). Her poetic voice contrasts the dark sadness within with vivid colors of life and happiness without—the blue sky, the sparkling green fields. Green usually symbolizes hope and renewal; however, in her view of human existence as radical insufficiency, Castro responds gloomily to this color as she has lost her faith in God and eternal life. Her lack of religious beliefs has turned the world into a wretched place: "para el alma desolada y huérfana/no hay estación risueña ni propicia" (*Sar* 467, for the orphaned and desolate soul/there is no happy nor sunny season). Castro sadly perceives herself as a spiritual orphan. She implies that as the religious flame burns out, so too does the vital force of human life (*Sar* 481). The human being's doubts about the afterlife can only be resolved by dying (*Sar* 495).

Castro's spiritual crisis has great impact on her writing. She confesses that she wrote *Follas novas* "en medio de tódolos desterros" (271, in exile). She refers not only to exile in a physical sense, as she wrote these verses mostly in Castile, but also in a spiritual sense, that is, in exile from God. She affirms that the leaves of her book are limp because they express feelings of spiritual alienation (278–279), and her verses, infected by her loss of faith, are bitter (285–286). Her consistent use of sickness imagery when representing her religious skepticism reveals not only her lack of psychic wholeness but also the debilitating effect of her loss of faith on her: "a alma enferma, poeta e sensibre,/que todo a lastima,/que todo lle doi" (*Follas novas* 357, a soul sick and sensitive,/which everything hurts,/which everything pains). Castro's religious dilemma influences not only the substance of her writing but the form as well. She suggests that in her poetry, ideas haphazardly spark in the darkness as she gropes for meaning in the radical insufficiency of human life. The unconventional harmony and structure of her poems spring, therefore, in a spontaneous manner from her religious doubts and genuine searching for God like breezes "que neste mundo triste/o camiño do ceu buscan perdidas" (*Follas novas* 278, that in this sad world/lost they seek the heavenly path).

Like Castro, Silva is unable to reconcile human suffering, such as the death of innocents, with the existence of God (*De sobremesa* 245–246).[3] Indeed, he likens the disillusionment of life to an open wound (*Intimidades* 161). His readings in philosophy and science further diminish his religious faith by leading him to reduce existence to nothing more than a conglomeration of atoms, governed by natural laws (*De sobremesa* 246). Yet like Castro he acknowledges that people confronted by the mystery and finality of death often desperately attempt to seek refuge in religion. On the death of his beloved grandmother his protagonist Fernández cries out in the pain and disenchantment of adulthood: "(Dios de mi infancia, si existes, sálvame!" (*De sobremesa* 270, God of my childhood, if you exist, save me!). Fernández also tries to attain a sense of spiritual peace through his amorous ideal, Helena, whom he elevates to a deity in the emptiness and unintelligibility of life that overwhelm him. As Orjuela indicates, Helena represents "el ansia de alcanzar un absoluto espiritual y, en sentido cristiano, la salvación del alma" (1976: 29, the desire to reach a spiritual absolute and, in the Christian sense, the salvation of the soul). But in the end Fernández sees Helena, who dies, as merely a poignant dream (350).

In contrast to Castro, Silva more consistently stresses his religious doubts and does not represent his struggle to maintain his faith. Instead, he portrays the traumatic emotional and psychological consequences of his loss of religious belief. His protagonist and alter ego never revives the faith of his childhood and painfully acknowledges that he lives an existence devoid of meaning. In the realms of death and religion Silva comes to accept as valid only what he directly observes. For instance, his poetic voice in "Poeta, di paso" (Poet, Say Softly) hears prayers of mourners, as if from a distance, revealing the remoteness of religious faith. Furthermore, these prayers are monotonous, useless in the face of death. The only tangible truth are the dead beloved's lips, frozen and purple (*Libro de versos* 29). He implies that death is the termination of physical life, and this is all that human beings can affirm with certainty.

As a corollary to their religious doubts, Silva and Castro express misgivings about the existence of an afterlife. Both refer to heaven as a dream. Silva represents how people fruitlessly dream about the afterlife, which he cynically reduces "a polvo imperceptible de Quimeras" (*Poesías varias* 115, to the imperceptible dust of a Chimera). The reduction of religious belief to dust reinforces the idea of death, disintegration, and the nothingness that follows. Castro's poetic voice, meanwhile, contemplates a winter scene from a window and wishes earnestly that the winter of life foreshadowed dreams of an eternal spring in heaven (*Sar* 489–490). A difference in tone is evident between Silva and Castro as they portray human dreaming about the hereafter. Silva, less yielding about his religious doubts, expresses pessimism about dreaming in vain, whereas Castro's tone is wistful as she sorrowfully recognizes the uncertainty of the afterlife. Castro reflects that beauty in the world—the light of dawn, the roar of the sea, the murmuring wind in the pines—is meaningless for those who do not believe in heaven, as such sublime experiences promise nothing after death (*Follas novas* 315). She compares dying to falling into a dark well "en donde/nunca o que cai se levanta" (*Follas novas* 283, where/what falls never rises). Such imagery lends a sense of frightened helplessness to her conviction that death is simply a termination of life without hope of salvation. Similarly, Silva represents the grave as merely an abyss: "También en el sepulcro helada sima/Más tarde dormiremos" (*Intimidades* 154, Also in the icy pit of the sepulchre/Later we shall sleep). In fact, Silva grows increasingly pessimistic about the possibility of eternal reward in an afterlife. Though in his earlier works he sounds a note of hopeful inquiry about heaven, deep pessimism later takes over. In his youthful poem "Crisálidas" (Cocoons) the golden butterfly represents the dead girl's soul, and the garden paradise. Although this poem has an element of religious skepticism, it also leaves open the possibility that an afterlife may exist: "[¿] Al dejar la prisión que las encierra/Qué encontrarán las almas?" (*Libro de versos* 10, When they leave the prison that has held them/What will the souls find?). However, by the time Silva writes "Una noche" his pessimism about the afterworld had deepened considerably. Here, he relates cold night air to the icy truth of nonbeing with the death of a young woman: "Era el frío del sepulcro, era el frío de la muerte,/Era el frío de la nada..." (*Libro de versos* 33, It was the cold of the tomb, it was the cold of death,/It was the cold of nothingness..."). Through mechanical repetition Silva's poetic voice displays shock at her sudden death. Ellipsis graphically reinforces the nothingness of death and the speaker's infinite agony. In "Una noche" death is a final separation without the possibility of reunion in an afterlife. Silva can only fruitlessly attempt to defy the painful truth of death through empty wish fulfillment, fantasy in gossamer shadows that come together by moonlight (*Libro de versos* 33). Camacho Guizado comments that the joining of the shadows "se realiza en el mundo de la fantasía sin ninguna concesión racionalista" (1968: 123, takes place in the world of fantasy with no concession to reason). Silva and Castro often reflect on the immortality of the human soul. Ultimately, however, they recognize that their questions remain unanswered (*Sar* 464; *Gotas amargas* 75).

Anxiety over the Passage of Time and Death

Once Castro and Silva acknowledge the uncertainty of the afterlife, they grapple with the concept of human mortality. If death is definitive and complete, with no beyond, then people must live their lives subject to a deadline. This deadline is itself uncertain, however, because death may occur unexpectedly. Castro and Silva therefore experience a sense of restlessness and time pressure. For these writers ringing bells do not give the time but cruelly take it away (*Follas novas* 301–302; *Libro de versos* 68). When both poets represent the confrontation of past and present, they express an irrevocable sense of loss. Their world is not intact anymore as people they once knew have passed away, perhaps into nothingness. In one poem Castro's poetic voice visits places that recall the loss and absence of deceased beloveds, making her feel like a foreigner in her homeland and evoking her chilling cry, "*¡Padrón!... ¡Padrón!/Santa María ... Lestrove.../¡Adios! ¡Adios!*" (*Follas novas* 312, Padrón! ... Padrón!/Santa María ... Lestrove.../Good-bye! Good-bye!) Castro's recognition of the passage of time often results in an elegaic lament:

Aquelas risas sin fin,
aquel brincar sin dolor,
aquela louca alegría,
¿por que acabou?
Aqueles doces cantores,
aquelas falas de amor,
aquelas noites serenas,
¿por que non son?
Aquel vibrar sonoroso
das cordas da arpa i os sons
da guitarra malencónica,
¿quen os levou?
Todo é silensio mudo,
soidá, delor,
onde outro tempo a dicha
sola reinou.... (*Follas novas* 312)

That endless laughter,
that playing without pain,
that mad happiness,
why did it end?
Those sweet songs,
those words of love,
those serene nights,
why no more?
Those resounding vibrations
of the ancient harps and the melody
of the nostalgic guitar,
who stole them?
Everything is mute silence,
pain, suffering,
where before happiness
only reigned....

Castro's poetic voice relegates lack of suffering to a past full of laughter, play, happiness, song, music, and love. The shortness of the tetrasyllables

(4, 8, 12) contrasts with the octosyllables to reinforce the startling and incomprehensible discrepancy between past and present. Nighttime, often associated with death and uncertainty, was consistently serene in the past. The joyful and harmonious sounds of yesterday starkly oppose the silence and pain of the present. "Silensio" (silence) in line 13, intensified by the adjective *mudo* (mute), becomes a shocked silence, and repetition throughout increases pathos by displaying vain attempts to reconcile the harshness of today with pleasant memories of the past. In the radical insufficiency of existence Silva also underscores how pain often enters human life as time elapses: "Van, con rapidez que asombra,/Amigos al cementerio/Ilusiones a la sombra" (*Libro de versos* 57, They go, with amazing speed,/Friends to the cemetery/Dreams to the shadows).

For the two authors nature often possesses symbolic significance frequently referring to death.[4] Changing seasons become a painful reminder of human transience. Castro projects her fear of death through autumn leaves that tremble on bare branches (*Sar* 494). Silva perceives the fall landscape as a symbol of all that has gone before and no longer exists (*Libro de versos* 56). In their representation of the eternal renewal of nature and their own perishability these authors express the agony of human consciousness (*Sar* 526; *Intimidades* 179). Fearing death, yet lacking confidence in an afterlife, Castro sometimes desperately wishes to share the permanence of the natural world and "girar con los astros por el celeste piélago" (*Sar* 527, to revolve with the stars in the celestial space). The impossibility of her desire for permanence increases her despair:

> Natureza fermosa,
> a mesma eternamente,
> dille ós mortais, de novo ós loucos dille
> ¡que eles no máis perecen! (*Follas novas* 297)
>
> *Beautiful nature,*
> *eternally the same,*
> *tells mortals, tell those crazy creatures*
> *that only they die!*

Through personification Castro actually contrasts nature to humankind to suggest that only humans die, never to return. Exclamation marks in the final verse enclose the frustration and pain of her poetic voice.

For both writers, as in Bécquer, the swallow, a harbinger of spring, portrays the pathos of the inexorable flow of time (*Sar* 493–494; *Poesías varias* 106–107).[5] Castro and Silva repeatedly present images of the rapid passage of time as a constant reminder of human ephemerality. Castro emphasizes transience through flowers and plants: "La que ayer fue capullo, es rosa ya,/y pronto agostará rosas y plantas/el calor estival" (*Sar* 466, The bud of yesterday, is a rose today,/and soon roses and plants will dry/in the heat of summer). Silva declares that the hour bell "sigue marcando con el mismo modo/El mismo entusiasmo y el mismo desgaire/La huida del tiempo que lo borra todo!" (*Libro de versos* 68, continues marking in the same way/With the same enthusiasm and with the same disregard/The flight of time that erases all!). Repetition of the word *mismo* (same) emphasizes the unalterable progression of time, signaling human transitoriness. Likewise, in these lines Castro presents the perpetual swinging of a pendulum as menacing:

> ¡Tas-tis!, ¡Tas-tis!, na silenciosa noite
> con siniestro compás repite a péndola,
> mentras a frecha aguda,
> marcando un i outro instante antre as tiniebras,
> do relox sempre imóbil
> recorre lentamente a limpa esfera. (*Follas novas* 307)
>
> *Tick-tock!, Tick-tock!, in the silent night*
> *rhythmically intones the sinister pendulum,*
> *while the sharp arrow,*
> *marking each instant in the darkness*
> *on the perpetually still clock*
> *slowly courses the impassive face.*

Onomatopoeia in line 1 increases tension and contrasts against the silence of the night. As in Silva's "Día de difuntos" (*Libro de versos* 64–68), time appears indifferent to its relentless, unvarying course. In another poem Castro affirms that "Os homes pasan, tal como pasa/nube de vran" (*Follas novas* 309, Men pass away, as pass/the summer clouds). Her simile expresses considerable pessimism about human life, destructible, insubstantial, fleeting. As she continues to consider the brevity of human life in the same poem, she contrasts stone statues with mortals who suffer and live under the fearful shadow of death. Fervently she wishes she were like those insensitive statues, not subject to the laws of change, decay, and death:

> I as pedras quedan ... e cando eu morra,
> ti, Catredal,
> ti, parda mole, pesada e triste,
> ¡cando eu non sea, ti inda serás! (*Follas novas* 309)

The stones remain ... and when I die,
you, Cathedral,
you, dark mass, heavy and sad,
when I am no longer, you still will be!

In a thematically similar poem Silva juxtaposes the permanence of a colonial window with human mortality. He imagines the forgotten generations that have looked out to the world through the window—a colonial judge, a dark-eyed Spanish beauty who misses her native Andalusia, and now a group of rosy-cheeked children. As an opening the window symbolizes eternity, where past, present, and future merge:

...Tal vez mañana,
Cuando de aquellos niños queden sólo
Las ignotas y viejas sepulturas
Aún tenga el mismo sitio la ventana. (*Intimidades* 193)

...Perhaps tomorrow,
When all that is left of those children
Are forgotten and old tombs
The window will be in its same place.

Both authors frequently employ the moon not only as a symbol of the ever-presence of death in human existence but also as a measure of human transience. Castro's poetic voice affirms of the moon, "¡de cuántos, que dichosos ayer la contemplaron,/alumbrarán la tumba sus rayos transparentes!" (*Sar* 494, of how many, who in happiness looked at it yesterday,/its transparent rays will illuminate their tombs!) In Silva's "Una noche" the moon creates two delicate shadows as lovers walk together, and then, upon the death of the young woman, projects only one shadow: "¡Iba sola por la estepa solitaria!" (*Libro de versos* 33, Alone traversing the solitary steppe!) In Silva's "Luz de luna" (*Libro de versos* 53–55, Moonlight) and Castro's "Quisiera, hermosa mía" (*Sar* 503–508, I Would Like, Beautiful One), both on the brevity of human love, the rays of the moon represent both the constancy of death in human life and the ironic permanence of vague, transparent, empty moonbeams against the caducity of the human being. Repeatedly they underscore the awe and mystery that death eternally inspires in the human being.

For Castro and Silva the ever-present threat of death prompts people to contemplate ways of overcoming it. Such attempts prove futile, however. Both authors show how material possessions become pathetic symbols of human pride as the possessions, rather than the people, are all that ultimately survive (*Cantares gallegos* 624–625; *Libro de versos* 39-40). Castro and Silva thus counterpose with sorrow the permanence of objects with human fragility. Schulman appropriately notes that for a pessimist such as Silva, "el tiempo sólo se concibe en términos de un inútil esfuerzo humano—*vanitas vanitatum*—abocado con la amenaza constante de la muerte" (192, time can only be conceived in terms of futile human efforts—*vanitas vanitatum*—shadowed by the constant threat of death). The same applies to Castro.

Both poets most clearly express their anguish about the circumscription of human life to time when they note how death may unexpectedly strike the young.[6] For Castro, as for Silva, death emerges as the most graphic symbol for the irrational nature of life. Throughout her works Castro ironically juxtaposes the young who die with the old who live: "Sucumbe el joven, y encorvado, enfermo,/sobrevive el anciano" (*Sar* 536, The young man succumbs, and hunched, sick,/the old man survives). In another poem, as it softly rains, her poetic voice laments the death of her young child (*Sar* 463).[7] In this poem, as in others, Castro vividly contrasts the pain of death for the living and the insensitivity of the deceased. She also frequently portrays how forced emigration tragically results in death for many people still in their prime (*Follas novas* 407). Indeed, she movingly expresses the anxiety of the Galician emigré who fears dying in foreign lands: "Non permitás que aquí morra,/airiños da miña terra" (*Cantares gallegos* 549, Do not let me die here,/breezes of my land). In another poem Castro's poetic voice angrily recounts how her beloved lost his life in the severe and arid land of Castile where poverty forced him to earn a living (*Cantares gallegos* 598).

Silva also presents images of premature death, usually involving young, beautiful women. In one poem the red lips of an adolescent girl who has died, still vividly recall pulsing blood and life (*Intimidades* 202). In another poem, "Poeta, di paso," a woman of twenty dies unexpectedly (*Libro de versos* 28). The poetic voice provides no reason for her death or for that of the young woman in "Una noche" (*Libro de versos* 32–33), and none is expected; death, particularly when it assails the young, defies logic.[8] For both authors death is not only uncertain but often cruel. Silva contrasts the permanence of a statue of Bolívar with the mortality of children who play close by (*Libro de versos* 24). To support his view of existence as radical insufficiency, Silva depicts a startling number of children who die and many who are sickly, thereby emphasizing the fragility and uncertainty of human life (*Libro de versos* 7, 10; *Intimidades* 156, 202). These authors also morbidly describe death and its funereal trappings in vivid detail, thus displaying their own horror and fear of death. Echoing the medieval *Danza de la muerte* (Dance of Death) Castro portrays worms that gnaw a decaying body under an elegant marble tombstone (*El caballero de las botas azules* 15–16). In "La recluta" (The Recruit) Silva depicts a fallen soldier with grisly verisimilitude. The soldier's open eyes may symbolize final understanding of the meaninglessness of life—and death (*Poesías varias* 104).

With characteristic pessimism Castro and Silva sadly observe how the death of an individual's memory on earth may accompany biological death. Attempts to attain immortality through the memories of the survivors prove unfulfilling because of the uncertainty that memories will last. Castro's poetic voice ironically contrasts the noisy lamentations of mourners with the ear-splitting silence that so shortly follows the deceased into the grave and into oblivion (*Sar* 538). The brevity of another poem stylistically reinforces Castro's theme that the dead are often hurriedly buried and forgotten. To emphasize the idea of submergence, she repeats the word *cava* (dig) five times and modifies *burato* (hole) with the adjective *fondo* (deep). Burying a memory parallels burying the dead. Through personification Castro poignantly reinforces the personal initiative involved in the act of forgetting. Yet she also uses the imperative repeatedly as if to suggest the difficulty of forgetting:

> Cava lixeiro, cava,
> xigante pensamento,
> cava un fondo burato onde a memoria
> do pasado enterremos.
> ¡Á terra cos difuntos!
> ¡Cava, cava lixeiro!
> E por lousa daraslle o negro olvido,
> i a nada lle darás por simiterio. (*Follas novas* 303)
>
> *Dig lightly, dig,*
> *giant thought,*
> *dig a deep hole and the memory*
> *of the past let us bury.*
> *The dead to the earth!*
> *Dig, dig lightly!*
> *For a marker you will give it utter oblivion,*
> *nothingness you will give it for a tomb.*

The bitter tone of this poem echoes throughout her works when she treats the transitoriness of all things human. Indeed, Castro frequently displays anger because of the uncertainty, injustice, and limitations of life.

By contrast, Silva most commonly responds not with anger but with pain and despair. In the following poem the poetic voice conveys sadness in the desire to bury, intact, tender memories of a young woman who has recently died. The burial will protect memories of her, far from a harsh world. The steady octosyllabic rhythm may suggest that time endlessly erodes all things, including the memory of the young girl. As in Castro, repetition in lines 1 and 2 emphasizes the idea of interment and, ultimately, of obliteration:

Cavad ahora otra fosa,
Cavadla con mano trémula,
De la sonrïente niña
Del triste sepulcro cerca,
Para que lejos del mundo
Su sueño postrero duerman
Mis recuerdos de cariño
Y mis memorias más tiernas. (*Intimidades* 202)

Dig now this hole,
Dig it with a tremulous hand,
Of the smiling girl's
Sad tomb near,
So that away from the world
May lie in their last slumber
My remembrances of love
And my most tender memories.

Silva's "Día de difuntos" also acknowledges how the living forget the dead, even those who were once seemingly essential to their happiness. Silva's poetic voice sadly presents a daughter who prepares for a dance: "al año justo, un vestido aéreo,/Estrena la niña, cuya madre duerme/Olvidada y sola, en el cementerio" (*Libro de versos* 67, exactly a year later, a diaphanous dress,/The girl wears, whose mother slumbers/In the cemetery forgotten and alone). Similarly, the poetic voice describes how a widower spoke of suicide following his wife's death and then, silenced by sheer happiness, "A la misma iglesia fue con otra novia" (*Libro de versos* 67, To the same church he went with another sweetheart). Through the fugacity of human memory Silva represents the egotism of people of all ages and of both sexes.

Castro and Silva express anxiety not only about the possibility of biological and metaphysical death but also about the possible loss of personal identity through a psychological illness that may alter human personality, that is, "biographical death" (Laín, *Antropología* 154). In *Ruinas* Castro depicts Montenegro's derangement as a defense mechanism against accumulated feelings of powerlessness and alienation (727). To express that his life has dried up, Castro describes Montenegro drinking at every fountain as he roams the countryside until his premature death (727). She suggests through her portrayal of Montenegro that those who possess acutely sensitive natures are more susceptible to mental disease. Other characters who succumb to insanity because of severe psychological pressures and personal suffering include Luis of *El primer loco* and Candora, Fausto, and Esperanza of *La hija del mar*.

In her depiction of insanity Castro represents how dementia transforms the external circumstances of her characters; by contrast, Silva explores in detail the inner torment of encroaching mental disease through his protagonist. Fernández conceives insanity as a woman, that is, as a terrible temptress. Symbolizing a privation or a removal, she is a vivid manifestation of the radical insufficiency of human existence. Fernández envisions her dressed in shiny rags, her teeth chattering as she shakes the bells of a bizarre scepter and grimaces mysteriously, inviting him toward the unknown (*De sobremesa* 294). Rags graphically symbolize deep emotional wounds within Fernández's psyche. Teeth, as weapons of attack, represent his deep fear of mental illness. The scepter that Insanity wields is an emblem of the frightening power Fernández believes she possesses over him. Fernández focuses on Insanity's mouth, not only as a destructive force that devours but also as the point of contact between external and internal worlds. Fernández thus reveals his desire to communicate his desperate mental state. The meaninglessness and psychological isolation in which he lives, exacerbated by feelings of spiritual orphanhood, tragically lead to the pressures of mental instability (*De sobremesa* 270). For both Silva and Castro insanity is a form of severe alienation, a rejection not only of others but also a possible and fearful negation of intimate aspects of selfhood.

Failure of Hedonism to Provide Fulfillment

Uncertain about the meaningfulness of life even as radical insufficiency, and acknowledging the fragility of the human being, Castro and Silva at times express an angry and cynical attitude of hedonism. Castro, who attempts to cling to religious faith, adopts this stance reluctantly and with an overlay of guilt (*Sar* 510). Silva, who has irretrievably discarded religious faith, attempts more actively than Castro to use this attitude as an antidote to anxiety about earthly existence and an afterlife (*De sobremesa* 236). In fact, unlike Castro Silva openly condemns religious teachings as "peligrosas fantasías" (*Poesías varias* 115, dangerous fantasies) because they wrongly suppress a hedonistic mentality. His poetic voice advises the human being to seek "en perfumadas primaveras/todo el supremo bienestar, que esperas/del Cielo que prometes o que ansías" (*Poesías varias* 115, in sweet-smelling springs/all the supreme well-being, that you expect/from that heaven that you promise or that you anxiously desire). The softly alliterative *p* and the vernal imagery delicately tantalize. The truncation of this poem, the second of the "Sonetos negros" (*Poesías varias* 115, Dark Sonnets), also stylistically reinforces its carpe diem theme and the uncertainty of the future. In another poem Silva uses the image of a withered rose to advocate the enjoyment of youth and beauty because of their brevity (*Intimidades* 159–160).

Silva and Castro both depict the satisfaction of sexual urges as part of their disillusioned hedonism. In one of Silva's poems the white skull of a friar lies hidden in a convent garden. The wall of the garden, which is in ruins, may represent the tragic confinement of the ascetic life. The melancholy that Silva evokes in depicting the skull underscores the urgency of his *carpe diem* theme in the nothingness of death (*Poesías varias* 106–107). Repeatedly Silva exhorts the enjoyment of the flesh "antes de caer corrompida/en las negruras de la tierra!" (*Poesías varias* 114). In "Resurrexit" Silva further describes the tragic consequences of not being a hedonist. He likens the biblical Magdalen to Celestina as the go-between for dead spinsters alien to pleasure seeking. In the same poem Silva cynically insists that a stimulus to a guiltless attitude of *carpe diem* should be "el doliente recuerdo de un pasado/ cada vez más cercano y más distante" (*Gotas amargas* 94, the painful memory of a past/ever closer and ever distant). Through juxtaposition of the opposites *cercano* (closer) and *distante* (distant) the word *pasado* (past) comes to signify, ironically, both death and life. *Cercano* (Closer) refers to the imminency of death and *pasado* to death itself in the eventual passing away of the human being. *Distante* relates to the flow of time, which makes the "pasado" or sum total of a person's earthly existence ever more remote and nebulous. Because the human being will die physically and eventually in human memory, Silva pessimistically urges a life of enjoyment for the sake of delight in the absence of an afterlife.

Castro, however, is less adamant in espousing a *carpe diem* attitude.

She depicts, for instance, a poor, unhappy maiden who projects subconscious thoughts through the voice of Mephistopheles, thereby reflecting inner doubts about virtue, self-sacrifice, and divine reward. Privately, she wonders about the purpose of her austere lifestyle when considering the undeniability of death and the uncertainty of a heaven that may be pure fantasy (*Sar* 531–532). Both Castro and Silva ultimately reveal that a *carpe diem* attitude does not lead to fulfillment. For Castro the temptation of hedonism ultimately serves to highlight the intensity of her religious struggle, the uncertainty of God's existence, as well as her insatiable desire to find meaning in life. The decision of Silva's protagonist Fernández to embrace a *carpe diem* lifestyle results in a dispersal of energy in so many different directions that he ignores his writing and accomplishes nothing. Although he fully recognizes the emptiness of such a life, he continues his pursuit of endless pleasure as he cynically and conclusively accepts that existence lacks meaning (*De sobremesa* 233). Therefore, the inability of pleasure seeking to satisfy the human being's craving for meaning or to quiet anxiety in the radical insufficiency of human existence further emphasizes the emptiness and futility of human endeavor (*Follas novas* 363–364; *De sobremesa* 231.

The Longing for Death as Release

Beset by religious doubts, unable to find satisfaction in pleasure, and weary of earthly suffering, Castro and Silva see themselves as tired travelers and death as the only possible liberation. Although the afterlife is uncertain, Castro and Silva embrace death because it will at least end their radical insufficiency, their suffering on earth. For these authors the color gray prevails in the world, giving expression to feelings of depression, inertia, and indifference as a result of their view of human life as existential privation (*Sar* 489; *Libro de versos* 64). The considerable juxtaposition of light and dark imagery throughout Castro's and Silva's works essentially defines the source of their pessimism: the light or the possibility of happiness is what ultimately magnifies the dark shadows of life. Both portray world-weariness in the young who reject the suffering of existence (*Follas novas* 355; *Poesías varias* 100). In the absence of happiness and hope, in the monotony and emptiness of life, these authors express a yearning for death. For Castro and Silva death is, as for Schopenhauer, just a cessation of the pain of living. In a devastatingly pessimistic poem,

Castro declares "soio é remedio a morte/para curar da vida" (*Follas novas* 426, death is the only remedy/for life). She sensitively affirms that those who have had only good fortune may not understand the unfortunates who seek eternal forgetfulness (*Sar* 475). Throughout her own life she has felt segregated from the rest of humanity, suffering more than most and yearning in vain for peace: "Paz, paz deseada:/Pra min, ¿onde está?" (*Follas novas* 280, Peace, peace so desired: /For me, where is it?) Now she views death as the unconsciousness for which she longs.[9] Her poetic voice impatiently desires the new leaves of spring to arrive, urging "nelas deixá que o sono/eu durma do no ser" (*Follas novas* 352, that I may sleep amid them/the dream of not being).

Silva also displays despondency because death is the only possible remedy for the radical insufficiency of existence. In one ironic poem Christ raises a joyful Lazarus, who only four days later weeps out of envy for the dead (*Libro de versos* 52). In another poem bronze bells remind the poetic voice of the deceased, who are fortunate to be free of a world conceived in Schopenhaur's terms: "duermen ahora/Lejos de la vida, libres del deseo,/Lejos de las rudas batallas humanas!" (*Libro de versos* 66, now they slumber/Far from life, free from desire,/Away from the harsh human battle!) Similarly, Silva's novelistic character and alter ego, Fernández, wishes to dull his suffering: "Quería huir de la vida por una horas, no sentirla" (269, I wanted to flee from life for some hours, not to feel it). Fernández concludes that death offers him his only opportunity to escape the uncertainty and persistent anxiety inherent in living. In his despair he admits that there are times when, incapable of the most minimal effort, he calls plaintively for death "ya que la energía no me alcanza para acercarme a la sien la boca de acero que podría curarme del horrible, del tenebroso mal de vivir..." (293–294, as I do not have the energy to raise to my temple the steel rod which could cure me from the terrible, dismal disease of living...). Like Castro in her *Follas novas* poem (426), Silva pessimistically refers to death as a cure for life. In both cases the poets express a euthanasic attitude toward death because of the incessant suffering of life.

Not surprisingly, both authors have a distinctly positive view of suicide. Castro consistently depicts suicide as a reasonable and legitimate means of deliverance. She sincerely wonders why suicide is considered a crime when human beings long merely to end their martyrdom on this earth (*Follas novas* 315–316; *Sar* 550–551). Critics have particularly remarked on Castro's fascination with the sea and suicide (Poullain, 1974: 148). In one poem murmuring waves entice the poetic voice just as sirens lure the wayfarer with their song of intense sweetness.[10] The mythological allusion reinforces Castro's desire for self-destruction (*Follas novas*

285). Her novelistic character Esperanza commits suicide by drowning, desperately seeking solace in death. Her tomb is the sea "que el humano pie no huella jamás" (*La hija del mar* 216, where the human foot never steps); that is, she cannot be hurt by life any longer. Repeatedly, Castro—and Silva—yearn only for senselessness without any mention or hope of metaphysical resurrection.

Suicide themes are also common in works by Silva, but unlike Castro he dwells less on suicide as a topic for debate than on the act itself.[11] His character Juan de Dios is thoroughly bored, bitter, and disenchanted with life; impulsively "se curó para siempre con las cápsulas/De plomo de un fusil" (*Gotas amargas* 78, he cured himself forever with the pills/Of lead from a rifle). In "Zoospermos" (Sperm) a scientist recklessly proclaims that one of the spermatozoids "se hubiera suicidado" (*Gotas amargas* 85, would have committed suicide) with a Smith and Wesson revolver.[12] For Silva suicide is a response to the pain and disillusionment of life. Sometimes he presents suicide as premeditated (*De sobremesa* 293–294) and other times as precipitous (*Gotas amargas* 78), but never as censurable.[13] Indeed, his valedictory address, *De sobremesa*, is mostly monologue and reflects Silva's growing detachment and rejection of the inescapable anxiety of life. In the case of both authors, apprehension frequently stems not from leaving this world but from not knowing when they will leave it. Persistently they display a thematic attraction to the cemetery as a repository for the weary flesh (*Libro de versos* 63; *Poemas sueltos* 588–589, Mixed Poems).[14]

Conclusion

An unrelenting concern with death distinguishes the writings of Castro and Silva. Uppermost in their minds is the idea of change and death as the basic characteristic of existence. The thought that death may be better than the suffering inherent in life finds eloquent expression in their works. They conclude that whatever peace humans can attain in the face of their suffering and the recognition of the futility of life, comes from the liberation promised by death. Therefore, Castro and Silva do not fear death but rather look on it as a release. In coming to this conclusion they have struggled with the most central questions of human existence, namely, the purpose of human suffering and whether God and an afterlife exist. The ways they approach these questions reflect not only the era in which they lived but also their own personal development. In their writing they explore the questions of human life and death in the context of two systems: religious faith and reason. On the one hand, the Catholic tradition of their childhood offers blind faith as the answer to their questions surrounding the mystery of life and death. However, their intelligence cannot reconcile earthly suffering with a compassionate God, whom they attempt to understand rationally. Generally Castro is less intellectualistic in her metaphysical inquiry than Silva, who mentions specific philosophers and philosophies, lending at times a more coldly analytical texture to his writings. Both poets show, however, that reason alone is insufficient to plumb the depths of the questions they pose. They are therefore left ultimately with an abiding uncertainty and a deep despair at failing to make human life intelligible. Death becomes for them the only possible answer to the radical insufficiency of human existence.

CONCLUSION

The foregoing study has proved that radical insufficiency lies at the heart of the worldviews of R. de Castro and J. A. Silva. This conception, an original synthesis of the philosophies of Ortega, Zubiri, and Laín Entralgo, has made it possible for the first time to attempt a rigorous comparison of the lyric voices of Castro and Silva, whose works transcend classification as merely regional literature. There exist between them astonishing similarities of themes, tones, and images, along with differences that display each artist's personality. Neither author conforms to the artistic, intellectual, religious, and cultural paradigm of society. Each reveals instead the misgivings, instability, and fear of an age in spiritual and moral crisis because of rapid political, social, and technological change. Both writers come to acknowledge human existence as the experience of radical insufficiency: (1) They show how humans lack a determined being and fixed course or destiny for life. In their works, eternal norms are unavailable to them to guide conduct and to make the world intelligible. As a result, humans experience feelings of uncertainty and emptiness that inevitably lead to anxiety. Castro and Silva write of their own unsuccessful endeavors to find a solution to the radical insufficiency of life. (2) Confronted by the uncertainty of human existence, both authors describe futile attempts to overcome radical insufficiency through the creation and contemplation of art. Yet art does not provide solace precisely because of unpredictability with regard to artistic production, reception, and perdurability. (3) Castro and Silva also reveal that attempts to attain fulfillment and direction through love are as fraught with pitfalls as is art. They emphasize the inadequacy of human relationships as sources of stability and orientation as they systematically strip away idealizations about romantic love. (4) Last, they acknowledge the failure of religion to supply guidance and reassurance. They view religion as problematic because of the inherent uncertainty surrounding the existence of God and an afterlife.

These authors try to convey the deep-reaching tragedy of existence with all its privations and establish that humans must create their own lives, with nothing to direct them except their own experience. Both recognize faith and science as systems providing security in the past. They also agree that, lacking an eternal human nature, people change over time. Although this mutability implies that humans are free to achieve the greatest heights of self-realization, Castro and Silva pessimistically suggest that people often cannot fulfill their potential and objectives because of limitations resulting from their particular life circumstances. Castro indicates how prejudicial attitudes inhibit women who attempt to pursue literary careers. In addition, she eloquently describes the plight of the poor, especially the tragic physical and psychological consequences of forced Galician emigration. For his part, Silva writes of constraints on self-affirmation arising from the deficient artistic, cultural, and intellectual level of Colombian bourgeois society and pressures toward mindless conformity. These limitations and anxieties cause both authors to display an impossible wish to escape life through dreams, though Silva is more insistent in this theme than is Castro. In general, the two writers affirm that people grow increasingly pessimistic over time as they encounter disillusioning life experiences. As a result, both authors dwell on memories of happier days of childhood and adolescence. For Silva memory only fleetingly recaptures the innocence of childhood; Castro depicts remembrance as a painful contrast between the blissful ignorance of childhood and bitter maturity.

The anxiety that fills Castro and Silva in response to the uncertainty and limitations of life inspires them to write. Indeed, Castro asserts that her suffering is the source of her inspiration. Silva views the desire to beautify harsh experience as the stimulus for writing. For both poets artistic production serves as the vehicle by which they attempt to gain control and create meaning in the radical insufficiency of existence. However, they reveal that art is inadequate in this regard: either the artist lacks talent, or the public may not understand or accept the artist's subjective perception. Castro represents misgivings about her own talent as a writer. She thereby reflects her lack of self-assurance and her absorption of negative social views toward female writers (although at other times her trepidation is conciliatory in nature to undermine censorship in a patriarchal society). Unlike Castro, Silva does not display insecurity about his artistic abilities; instead, he reveals dissatisfaction with the public's lack of critical perception in the judgment and appreciation of art. Both writers concur, however, in deploring the inherent deficiencies of language itself as an artistic medium. Nevertheless, even if these difficulties of language could be overcome, art still could not rise above the radical insufficiency of existence because art is itself only a projection of the imperfect human being. It does not provide Castro or Silva with guidance or security.

As with art, romantic love, according to these authors, cannot prevail over radical insufficiency. They insist that enduring love is often impossible to achieve because death intervenes, outside circumstances intrude, or their characters are psychologically incapable of sustaining such an emotion. Silva in particular highlights how death separates lovers, whereas Castro focuses on the devastating emotional effects of forced Galician emigration, especially on women. Both also reject the romantic notion of the intrinsic value of love by describing the suffering of unreciprocated love and the unfulfilling nature of carnal love. They point out as well that neither conjugal nor spiritual love provides security, direction, contentment, or a sense of completion in life. For these authors love, which they often portray as a deluded state, is frequently a source of anguish and unhappiness. Indeed, the romantic ideal of love provokes great suffering and disillusionment when contrasted with lived experience.

Castro and Silva also indicate that religious faith does not counter the radical insufficiency of existence. On the contrary, they describe the suffering they experience because of the uncertainty of religious beliefs. Both write about their religious doubts, which stem from their inability to reconcile rationally human suffering with the existence of God. Although these writers acknowledge and long for the comfort and guidance that they believe strong religious faith could provide, they are unable to overcome their skepticism. They reveal deep pessimism and anxiety as they recognize their abandonment in an uncertain world. Castro, however, does struggle at times to regain her lost faith, whereas Silva does not, concentrating instead on the grim psychological consequences of this doubt. As an extension of their religious misgivings, both authors also feel uncertainty about the afterlife. Indeed, both depict heaven as nothing more than a poignant human dream (though in her later writing Castro occasionally expresses hope that the afterlife may exist).

In the absence of any strong convictions about God's existence and the possibility of heaven, the passage of time and death assume for these authors a terrifying significance. Castro's and Silva's graphic depictions of death reflect this terror. They express anxiety about the uncertainty of when death will strike, often underscoring this anxiety by depicting the premature death of young people. Silva particularly describes the deaths of young, beautiful women. Moreover, these authors sadly note that physical death often implies the death of an individual's memory, portraying the uncertainty of achieving earthly immortality through artistic creation or the recollections of those who survive. As a result of this uncertainty about the timing of death and the existence of an afterlife, Castro and Silva sometimes recommend hedonism. Silva more fully espouses this attitude, however; Castro displays guilt because of her continuing religious struggle. For both, though, hedonism fails to supply fulfillment and becomes a pitiful symbol of human yearning for a belief system that provides a code of conduct and a means of comprehending existence. In the end, plagued by religious doubts and exhausted by their suffering, Castro and Silva cling to the only certain fact of existence—that death will end their earthly torment. Therefore, they often display a yearning for death as an end point despite the ambiguity of the afterlife. They also reveal a positive attitude toward suicide as a means of escaping the anxiety produced by the radical insufficiency of human life. Castro and Silva show that preconceptions about existence, art, love, and religious faith fail when confronted by their view of being human. In their writing they emphasize the distress that necessarily results from this conception as they portray with eloquence and honesty the terrifying mystery, limits, and pathos of human life.

Notes

Introduction

1. Most of Silva's work was published posthumously. Refer to Orjuela's introduction (1990: xxii–xxxiii) for a thoroughly researched publication history of Silva's oeuvre.

2. As writers, they inspired Rubén Darío, Juan Ramón Jiménez, and Antonio Machado (Aldaz 6–7; Kulp 26–27; Miramón 173, 178–179).

3. In tragic ways, too, their own lives were cut short. At thirty-one Silva shot himself in the heart, and Castro died slowly and painfully at forty-eight of uterine cancer (Kulp-Hill 29–30; Litvak 379).

4. Gonzalo Corona Marzol discusses themes and images essential to Castro introduced in *La flor*, 1857 (The Flower), and *A mi madre*, 1863 (To My Mother), that Castro fully develops in her later poetry. These brief volumes, although not discussed here as they are not representative of Castro's finest poetry, are helpful nonetheless to those who would attain a complete understanding of her artistic evolution.

5. An eloquent example of tragic happenstance is the shipwreck of L'Amérique on the Caribbean coast of Colombia in which Silva lost his *Cuentos negros* (Dark Stories), *Las almas muertas* (The Dead Souls), and *Los poemas de la carne* (Poems of the Flesh), which he considered his best works. The shipwreck may have been the result of a drunken bout of the captain's (de Brigard Silva, 1979: 727–728).

Chapter I

1. Childhood seems to have formed but a brief period of happiness in Castro's and Silva's own lives. Murguía probably refers to Castro's early

awareness of social reproach and curiosity as the illegitimate daughter of a priest and a woman of noble descent when he writes, "¡Y cuán amargos y tristes para los que, tocando apenas en los límites de la juventud, tienen ya que luchar con la tristísima realidad!" (1944: 137, How bitter and sad for those who, barely into their youth, have to fight already sad reality!). Silva, for his part, had trouble mixing with schoolmates. He was always conspicuous for his intellectual precocity and arrestingly elegant attire. His aloof demeanor and scrupulous manners earned him the nickname "José Presunción." Silva poignantly wished, however, to behave like other children his age:

> An introvert by nature, he compensated for his lack of communication with others by displaying his superior ability as a student. However, the intensity of his desire to be like the very children whom he exasperated is revealed in an anecdote portraying his excessive behavior when advised by a friend of the family to stop acting like an adult and to indulge in more childish pastimes, like throwing stones at the pigeons. A short time later, José Asunción was observed on the roof getting ready to throw an eleven-or-twelve-pound rock at the pigeons in the courtyard. (Osiek, 1978: 23)

Castro's and Silva's sensitivity and precociousness made them painfully aware of personal incongruency. In Silva's case, as he grew older he consciously cultivated idiosyncrasies in passive aggression against a world that disdained him and that he in turn disdained.

2. Related to the Spanish *soledad*, the word *saudade* derives from the Latin *solitatem* (Kulp-Hill 49). *Saudade* connotes sorrowful loneliness, nostalgia, and sad recollections. Kulp defines *saudade* as "one of the most Galician (and Portuguese) of sentiments. It is a complicated emotion, a longing for someone or something absent—for a parted loved one, for the dead, for the homeland or for happier former days" (144). See Ramón Piñeiro's article "A saudade en Rosalía" for a thorough treatment of this theme.

3. Unamuno discerningly wrote, "Tal vez se cortó Silva por propia mano el hilo de la vida por no poder seguir siendo niño en ella, porque el mundo le rompía con brutalidades el sueño poético de la infancia" (1979: 421, Perhaps Silva himself cut the thread of his own life because he could no longer continue to be a child as the world broke the poetic dream of childhood with its harshness). Unamuno has captured the essential tragedy of Silva's life. In his youth Silva was an idealist who truly believed in the fulfillment of hopes and dreams. As he continued to live, he grew unde-

ceived. His experience with creditors, including his own grandmother, affected him deeply. Continually the victim of adverse circumstances, Silva became a pessimist who could only look back longingly to simpler days. His tragic financial situation and constant retrospection defeated him.

4. For articles treating feminist perspectives see Matilde Albert Robatto, *Rosalía de Castro y la condición femenina* (1981, Rosalía de Castro and the Feminine Position) and Andrés Pociña, "La crítica feminista ante la obra de Rosalía de Castro" (Feminist Criticism and the Work of Rosalía de Castro) in *Crítica y ficción literaria: mujeres españolas contemporáneas* (1989, Criticism and Literary Fiction: Contemporary Spanish Women).

5. Murguía wrote the first critical article on Castro's work, titled "La flor, poesías de la señorita Rosalía de Castro" (The Flower, Poems of Miss Rosalía de Castro), published on May 12, 1857, in *La Iberia*, a Madrid newspaper. Murguía clairvoyantly wonders in his article whether Castro "ha nacido para ser algo más que una mujer, tal vez para legar un nombre honoroso a su patria" (Kulp-Hill 35, has been born to be more than a woman, perhaps to bequeathe an honorable name to her homeland). Critics dispute Murguía's claim that he was personally unacquainted with his future wife when he wrote his article (Mayoral, *Rosalía de Castro* 21–22). Although Murguía probably did know her when he evaluated *La flor*, this does not diminish his unusual perspicacity, especially when comparing the relative value of this first volume of poetry with Castro's later literary accomplishments.

6. In a letter to her husband we can clearly hear Castro's frustration with nineteenth-century parameters regarding female behavior: "Si yo fuera hombre, saldría en este momento y me dirigiría a un monte, pues el día está soberbio; tengo, sin embargo, que resignarme a permanecer encerrada en mi gran salón. *Sea.*" (*Cartas* 602, If I were a man, I would leave this minute and go to a mountain, as it is a beautiful day; I must, however, resign myself and remain cooped up in my grand parlor. So be it. *Correspondence.*)

7. Machado da Rosa affirms that Castro may have published *Las literatas* as a reaction to rumors that Murguía was helping her with her writing (74). Birute Ciplijauskaite puts Castro's literary woes in historical context: "Hay que recordar que en comparación con el resto de Europa, en la España de mediados del siglo XIX la mujer como creadora aún apenas estaba admitida" (323, It should be remembered that compared to the rest of Europe, in mid–nineteenth century Spain, women as creators were hardly accepted).

8. Castro herself as an adolescent attended a school sponsored by

the 'Sociedad Económica de Amigos del País' (Economic Society of Friends of the Region). Pérez affirms that the name of the school "implies low-cost schooling with emphasis on Galicia and things Galician" (31). It seems that Castro's education was actually rather scanty. Her preserved manuscripts are filled with spelling errors (Mayoral, 1974: 574). Murguía also confirms that Castro possessed "un temperamento por entero musical. De haber tenido una educación a propósito, hubiera sido una tan gran compositora como fue gran poeta" (1993, 449, a wholly musical temperament. Had she been educated differently, she would have become as great a composer as she was a poet). Through references and quotations in her first novel it is evident, though, that Castro read widely on her own.

Castro believed in promoting education for women. She encouraged young aspiring women authors (Carballo Calero 311), and in 1872 she went to live in Santiago so that her daughter Alejandra could perfect her drawing skills (Costa Clavell 80–81).

9. Certainly Silva's precarious financial situation limited his literary output. According to Miramón, Silva's mother blamed the family's continuing financial plight on Silva's penchant for writing: "El claro sentido mercantil de doña Vicenta sabía medir toda la gravedad de la situación, y desesperada en su escasez, achacaba los desastres al afán de Silva por los versos y a su afición a la lectura" (120, With her clear business sense doña Vicenta was able to gauge the seriousness of the situation, and desperate in her financial straits, blamed the disasters on Silva's love of verses and desire to read). However, doña Vicenta's grandson, Camilo de Brigard Silva, countered Miramón's assertion, affirming that his grandmother was supportive of her son in every way (Osiek, 1978: 34).

Silva's life truly became a financial nightmare following the death of his father on June 1, 1887. Silva wrote a one-hundred-page letter to Guillermo Uribe, his main creditor, explaining why he was unable to repay his debts. Uribe insisted, however, that Silva immediately repay both the business debts owed to him by his father and the money Silva had borrowed for such necessities as Elvira's funeral. Silva became involved in a long series of bankruptcy proceedings involving not only Uribe but other creditors. Ironically, Silva was not allowed to accept employment of any kind until all of the proceedings were terminated. According to Osiek,

> Uribe did not want to help Silva, and although he had been a long-time friend and business associate of his father he developed a violent antipathy toward the son of his old friend, and actually tried to harm him as much as he could. Not only did he use his influence to keep the debtors from agreement among themselves,

> but he was one of the first to notify the banks in Bogotá of Silva's likelihood of going broke, causing them to deny him the possibility of borrowing funds from them. (1978: 40–41)

10. As a sixteen-year-old witness to the horrific "Año del Hambre" (Year of the Famine) in Santiago in 1853, Castro reveals her empathy for the poor and hungry, which would become a distinguishing feature of her work. For moving testimony of this tragedy in Castro's own words, see Alonso Montero (1972: 19–20).

11. "La Choina," a childhood nurse of Castro's, taught her the songs and lore of Galicia (Kulp 2). Castro's dialect is from the shores of the Sar River, of Santiago de Compostela and the Amabia and Ulla River areas (Kulp 42). Courteau advances the interesting theory that Castro wrote her Spanish poetic texts with the intention of codifying Galician culture through Castilian by incorporating Celtic symbols and beliefs (1991: 87).

12. *Follas novas* first appeared in 1880 in Havana, where it was financed by Galician emigrés.

13. Born February 24, 1837, María Rosalita Rita was the illegitimate daughter of thirty-three-year-old María Teresa da Cruz y Abadía, who belonged to a family of minor Galician nobility, and of thirty-nine-year-old José Martínez Viojo, "variously termed seminarian, presbiter or priest" (Pérez 31). He later served as priest in Padrón. María Francisca Martínez, a faithful servant of her mother's, first cared for Castro until she went to live with her paternal aunts in Ortuño (Albert Robatto, 1995: 126). Although illegitimate children were relatively common in Galicia because of emigration (March 104), Castro felt the rejection of society as the product of a sacrilegious union. Castro lived under her mother's care when she was between the ages of ten and thirteen. The extent of her relationship with her father is unknown. According to José Filgueira Valverde, director of the museum of Pontevedra, there were those who told Castro's descendents how she would run at night to her father's door throughout her difficult life to ask him for help (189–190).

García Sabell and Rof Carballo emphasize, as do many critics, Castro's initial orphanhood when interpreting her works. According to García Sabell, Castro is "víctima de una ausencia irreparable—la del padre" (46, victim of an irreparable absence—that of the father). Rof Carballo adds that "la impresión más justa con la que puede resumirse la totalidad, el conjunto, de sus poesías es ésta: Son un gran vagabundaje, un merodeo en busca del rostro maternal, en busca de esa insaciada imagen arquetípica de la Madre, que es decisiva en la vida de todo hombre" (115–116, the most appropriate impression with which to summarize all her poetry is this: It is a broad wandering, a roaming in search of the maternal face, looking for that archetypical unsated image of the mother, which is decisive in the life of every man).

14. Silva's own genius was not recognized during his life or for years afterward. Lorenzo Marroquín, with the collaboration of José María Rivas Groot, atrociously satirized him in *Pax: Novela de Costumbres Latinoamericanas* (Pax: Novel of Latin American Customs). The 'Imprenta de la Luz' published the novel in Bogotá in 1907. One of the characters, S. C. Mata, was a clear caricature of Silva, whose name even mercilessly refers to the manner of Silva's death (Osiek, 1978: 45). The novel also contains an insensitive, vulgar parody of Silva's famous "Nocturno" (Nocturne), in which a monk commits suicide because he is afraid that he will succumb to the spell of a beautiful woman (McGrady 685–686).

15. Like Silva, Castro also shows feelings of being singled out and mocked. She compares malicious society to a pack of heartless dogs that pursue her incessantly: "Ladraban contra min, que camiñaba/casi que sin alento" (*Follas novas* 299, They were barking against me, who was walking/already almost out of breath, New Leaves). As with Silva she experiences alienation because of her propensity for introspection.

16. From the works lost in L'Amérique Silva reconstructed only *De sobremesa* at the fortunate insistence of his friend Hernando Villa (Orjuela, 1990: 441). Villa feared that Silva might be contemplating suicide (Miramón 161).

17. In addition to portraying religion and science as incapable of guiding humans, Silva and Castro also denounce positivism as a guiding philosophy. Silva criticizes the positivist Max Nordau and his scientific oversimplifications with regard to the judgment of art and the artist: "(Oh! grotesco doctor Max Nordau, si tu fe en la ciencia miope ha suprimido en ti el sentido del misterio" (*De sobremesa* 247, Oh! grotesque Doctor Max Nordau, your belief in myopic science has suppressed in you the sense of mystery). Castro also speaks against positivism as she comments on her century from a historical and literary standpoint, maintaining that "el positivismo mata el genio" (*La hija del mar* 78, positivism kills genius [Daughter of the Sea]).

18. Although Castro does refer to materialistic-minded priests (*Follas novas* 348), neither she nor Silva embrace anticlericalism as a theme. They continued to admire Christian ethics and respected always the faith of others.

Chapter II

1. In a letter to Colombian artist Rosa Ponce de Portocarrero Silva declares

> Es que usted y yo, más felices que los otros que pusieron sus esperanzas en el ferrocarril inconcluso, en el ministro incapaz, en la sementera malograda o en el papel moneda que pierde de su valor, en todo eso que interesa a los espíritus prácticos, tenemos la llave de oro con que se abre la puerta de un mundo que muchos no sospechan y que desprecian otros; de un mundo donde no hay desilusiones ni existe el tiempo; es que usted y yo preferimos al atravesar el desierto, los mirajes del cielo a las movedizas arenas, donde no se puede construir nada perdurable; en una palabra, es que usted y yo tenemos la chifladura del arte, como dicen los profanos, y con esa chifladura moriremos. (*Correspondencia* 681)
>
> *You and I, happier than those who put their hopes in the unfinished railroad, in the incompetent minister, in the harvest gone wrong or in paper money which loses its value, in all those things that are of interest to practical people, we possess the golden key that opens the door to a world unsuspected by many and despised by others; a world without disillusionments where time does not exist; you and I prefer when we cross the desert, the mirages of the sky to quicksand, where nothing permanent can be built; in a word, you and I possess the madness of art, as laymen say, and we shall keep that madness until we die.*

Silva thus acknowledges his need to create a beautiful, albeit false, world through art. Yet in the same letter he admits the difficulty involved in the creative act and the intrusions of the world. Tragically we know that art did not provide an *elixir vitae* for Silva. It was neither fulfilling nor meaningful enough to stay his hand from suicide. He would not live in abject poverty and lose face—not even to continue writing.

2. It is important to distinguish Castro's symbolic use of the term shadow and her popular use as a deceased soul that still inhabits the earthly world and maintains contact with living human beings. For a comprehensive treatment of the different kinds of shadows in Castro's works, see Mayoral's *La poesía de Rosalía de Castro* (1974).

3. Critical interpretations of Castro's "negra sombra" include a symbolic representation not only of existential anxiety but also of her illegitimacy, a bad memory, the sum total of life experience, human fear, and the uncertainty in existence (Courteau, 1995: 27–31).

4. Throughout Castro's works there is also evidence of gender-related trepidation regarding the explicitness of literary expression and thematic content. Both Castro and Silva describe sexual awakening, for instance, but in very different terms. Delicately Castro portrays a woman's loss of virginity: "entre las brumas/de la noche se pierde, y torna al alba,/ajado el velo" (*Sar* 470, amid the brume/of the night she gets lost, and returns at dawn,/her veil torn). Silva graphically depicts a young man's eagerly anticipated first sexual encounter with a prostitute, who infects him with a venereal disease, and his feelings of disillusionment (*Gotas amargas* 80). Silva's lack of hurtful confusion, pathetic justifications, and tentativeness about creating art provides vivid testimony, by contrast, of the circumscription to which nineteenth-century women writers were subject.

5. As is well known, Blanco Fombona advanced the theory that Silva and his sister Elvira were possibly incestuous lovers and utilized Silva's soulful writings for confirmation (451). Elvira's fiancé, however, was her cousin Julio Villar Gómez. Some biographers used this verifiable information to dispel rumors of an incestuous love affair (Orjuela, 1990: 434–435). Critics who have astonishingly accepted Blanco Fombona's theory include Alejandro C. Arias, Max Daireaux, Ricardo Gullón, and others (Osiek, 1978: 35–36). Although it is probably true that Silva was inspired to write "Una noche" in response to Elvira's death, his poem becomes far more universal and far-reaching in expression and meaning. Cuervo Márquez (495) advances the idea that Silva represents not Elvira but the Russian artist María Bashkirtseff in "Una noche," which I find difficult to accept given the raw and vital intensity of the poem.

6. Castro never complains in her poetry or novels about the pain she experiences associated with her cancer. Her personal pain, both physical and spiritual, brought her closer to suffering humanity, whereas Silva's material and spiritual suffering ultimately served to isolate him from others, culminating in suicide, an act not only of desperation but of alienation.

7. Silva never shared with his mother, younger sister, or closest friends his financial problems, which must have made his burden all the more difficult to bear. Silva's lack of openness also reveals how proud he was. Silva's nephew, Camilo de Brigard Silva, describes his uncle in the following manner: "Espíritu reconcentrado, quizá tímido, circunscrito al reducido círculo de su familia y de unos pocos amigos, sin confiar, sin embargo, a ninguno de ellos, ni sus angustias espirituales, ni sus preocupaciones materiales" (1965: 389, A soul in reverie, perhaps shy, circumscribed to the small circle of his family and a few friends, not confessing,

however, to any of them, neither his spiritual anguish, nor his financial worries). It would seem that Silva absorbed, to his detriment, nineteenth-century social expectations regarding masculine behavior that required the concealment of personal pain and hardship. Miramón notes that after the failure of Silva's polychromatic cement tile business, "Para mayor amargura, Silva tenía que continuar haciendo vida mundana" (150, To add to his anguish, Silva had to continue with his daily routine). The evening before Silva's suicide, friends came to a social gathering organized by his mother and sister. During this supper, "El último en ocupar un puesto, como era de cortesía fue José Asunción, quien se mostraba locuaz y salpicaba su charla con apuntes de fino humor. Esa era una de sus características: No dejar aflorar al exterior lo que escondía en sus adentros" (Serrano Camargo 209, The last one to sit at the table, as if by courtesy bound, was José Asunción, who was loquacious and sprinkled his conversation with fine humor. That was one of his characteristics: Never to allow what he was hiding inside to surface).

8. As with other poems, there is more than one rendition of this poem indicative of Silva's artistic uncertainty, conscientiousness, and desire for perfection. The first version is entitled "La musa eterna" (The Eternal Muse), dated October 6, 1883, and the corrected version, according to a note in the margin of the *Intimidades* manuscript is "A Diego Fallon" (To Diego Fallon). Orjuela (1990) includes all versions of Silva's poems.

9. According to Murguía, Castro's reply to critical injustices was: "Deja pasar todo; no somos más que sombra de sombras. Dentro de poco, ni mi nombre recordarán. Mas ¿esto qué importa a los que hemos traspasado nuestros límites?" (1993: 446, Let everything go; we are but a shadow of shadows. Soon, not even my name will be remembered. But what does that matter to those of us who have exceeded our limits?).

10. In a completely unrelated comment to a friend Silva curiously captures the essence of Castro's theme in *El caballero de las botas azules*, revealing his cynicism so clearly: "El brillo de las botas, créalo, es más importante que el de las ideas. Unas zapatillas de charol y una pechera blanca, ya tiene usted un hombre completo, seguro de triunfar en la sociedad" (Serrano Camargo 203, The shine on boots, believe me, is more important than that of ideas. Patent leather slippers and a white vest, and there you have a complete man, sure to succeed in society).

11. Castro's description of her poetic aspirations concurs with those of Bécquer:

> E nos dominios da especulación como nos do arte, nada máis inútil nin cruel do que o vulgar. Del fuxo sempre con todas as

miñas forzas, e por non caer en tan gran pecado nunca tentei pasar os límites da simple poesía, que encontra ás veces nunha espresión feliz, nunha idea afertunada, aquela cousa sin nome que vai direita como frecha, traspasa as nosas carnes, fainos estremecer, e resoa na alma dorida como un outra ¡ai! Que responde ó largo xemido que decote levantan en nós os dores da terra. (*Follas novas* 270–271)

And in the realm of speculation as in that of art, there is nothing more worthless or cruel than vulgarity. I shy away from it with all my might, not wishing to fall in that pit I never tried to exceed the limits of simple poetry, which finds at times in a good turn of phrase, in a lucky idea, that which unnamed, more straight than an arrow, pierces our flesh and, making us tremble, echoes in the aching soul as a new oh! That answers the long moan which the sufferings of the world awaken in us.

Similarly, Silva expresses the Bécquerian desire to create a poetry pregnant with suggestion: "Soñaba antes y sueño todavía a veces en adueñarme de la forma, en forjar estrofas que sugieran mil cosas oscuras que siento bullir dentro de mí mismo" (*De sobremesa* 232–233, I used to dream and still dream of mastering form, of composing stanzas to suggest a thousand vague things that I feel bubbling inside). Castro and Silva also coincide with Bécquer in representing the inability of language to express the most subtle human emotions.

12. In "Un poema" Silva describes how he chooses as his theme the death of a beautiful woman. Influenced by Poe's *The Philosophy of Composition*, Silva regarded this as the quintessential poetic theme and used it frequently throughout his works.

13. On her deathbed Castro insisted that all her unpublished manuscripts be destroyed. These included the prose works *Romana: provervio* (Romana: Proverb), *Cuentos extraños* (Strange Stories), and *Historia de mi abuelo* (History of my Grandfather) (Kulp 18–19). We can only speculate why Castro made this unusual request. Perhaps she felt she had not had the time to proofread and edit these works as she would have liked. Castro wrote her prose, unlike her intimate poetry, with an audience firmly in mind.

14. Castro could not have known at the time that her own book would far surpass Trueba's.

15. Murguía published Castro's first Galician poem "Adios, ríos; adios, fontes" in *El Museo Universal* on September 24, 1861, without her knowledge.

16. Two vivid examples of uncertainty regarding literary reception include the violent reaction toward Castro's story "El Codio" (Crust of Bread) and a passage contained in her article "Costumbres gallegas" (Galician Customs). On August 30, 1864, two hundred seminarians stoned the window of the press in Lugo, Soto Freire, where "El Codio," a story in which Castro criticized seminarians, was to be published. As a result, the story was lost (Alonso Montero, 1972: 55–56).

The reference to a sexual Galician custom in "Costumbres gallegas" resulted in a condemnation of Castro for what fellow Galicians claimed was erroneous information designed to disgrace Galicia. Very tactfully Castro describes an ancient custom in which people of the coast cordially permitted their women to stay with a lost or tired sailor for a night. Castro was so hurt by the vehemence of the public's outcry, which she rightfully considered unjust, that she vowed never to write in Galician again (Alonso Montero, 1972: 90–93).

17. Antolín Esperón Novás (1821–1895), lawyer, professor at the 'Instituto de Pontevedra' (*Institute of Pontevedra*), and literary censor, authorized the publication of Castro's *La hija del mar*. His letter addressed to Murguía is interesting as it conveys the thematic constraints imposed on authors of the time:

> Muy Sr. mío: en contestación a su apreciable digo a V. que por mí no hay inconveniente en que se continúe publicando la novela, cuya primera entrega tengo a la vista. Supongo que nada se hablará en ella de política ni de religión, lo que pudiera aparecer en falta del censor; pues su autora y lo que me dice el Sr. Compañel, son suficiente garantía. (Carballo Calero 307)
>
> *Dear Sir: In answer to your letter I inform you that I have no objection to continue with the publication of the novel, whose first proof I have here. I suppose that nothing will be said in it about politics or religion, as there will be no censoring; since the author and what Mr. Compañel said to me, pose sufficient guarantee.*

18. Luis Cernuda inaccurately blames Castro's slow critical acceptance exclusively on her bilingualism. He insists that "el motivo de la preterición no es que fuera mujer, como pensarán muchas feministas exacerbadas, sino acaso porque al escribir en gallego la mayor parte de sus versos, ella misma limitó el alcance de su obra" (61, the reason for her being kept in the background is not that she is a woman, as many exacerbated feminists will suppose, but perhaps because by writing in Galician she herself limits the dissemination of her work). The underestimation of

Castro's oeuvre was largely due to her gender because the Castilian *Sar* was not any better received than the Galician *Follas novas*. The literary hierarchy denied Castro, as a Spanish woman, the capacity to achieve successfully the metaphysical depth she clearly evinces in *Follas novas* and *Sar*. Tomayo y Baus presented a report on *Sar* in 1887 in the 'Real Academia Española' (*Royal Spanish Academy*) in which he disparagingly stated, representing the prevailing view of that institution, that *Sar* contained "no pocos deslices artísticos, extravagancias de forma y nebulosidades metafísicas que generalmente proceden del prurito de imitar la escuela germana, que no siempre están al alcance de la mujer española" (Davies, 1984: 616, not a few artistic slip-ups, extravagances in the form and metaphysical obscurities which generally come from the desire to imitate the German school, and which not always are within the reach of the Spanish woman).

19. Martínez Ruiz was among the first to expose the unmerited disregard Castro's work suffered at the hands of critics (37–38). Murguía, who was Castro's first critic, fought assiduously throughout his life for a fair appraisal of her work. In his "Cuentas ajustadas, medio cobradas" (Adjusted Accounts, Half Collected), published in *La Voz de Galicia* (The Voice of Galicia) in 1896, Murguía justifiably charged fellow Galician Pardo Bazán with intentionally overlooking Castro's work in her literary publications *Revista de Galicia* (1880, *Galician Review*), *Nuevo Teatro Crítico* (1891–93, *New Critical Theatre*), and in her 1896 article "La mujer española" (The Spanish Woman), in which she lauds Gómez Avellaneda, Carolina Coronado, Fernán Caballero, and Concepción Arenal while noticeably excluding Castro (Davies, 1984: 611–612; Varela Jácome, 1951: 413). Pardo Bazán allowed personal antipathy for what Castro represented as an intellectual to influence unjustly her judgment of Castro as an artist. Ironically, Pardo Bazán proclaimed in her address to the Lyceum of Artisans of La Coruña, held in honor of Castro on September 2, 1885, less than two months after her death, "Suele decirse que la hora de la muerte es de la justicia; no puede aplicarse al caso presente el axioma, puesto que en vida de Rosalía nadie desconoció sus méritos" (671, It is said that the hour of death is the hour of justice; the axiom cannot be applied to the present case, because during the life of Rosalía nobody was unaware of her merit). Nothing could have been further from the truth. In fact as further evidence of disregard, Castro's home was utterly abandoned until, in 1949, José Villar Granjel and José Mosquera Pérez bought it and donated it to the Castro Foundation. Agustín Sixto Seco interestingly points out the role Franco played in restoring Castro's home when, in 1969 the house was in ruins:

En el jardín pastoreaban las cabras. Los techos se hallaban sostenidos por clavos. En los suelos había botellas y tapas desperdigadas. Yo propuse ir a ver a Franco para intentar restaurar la vivienda. Le visité el 11 de octubre de 1970. Franco todavía se encontraba bastante bien. Nos dio luz verde y la casa-museo a que hoy todos pueden visitar se inauguró el 19 de agosto de 1972. (192–193)

In the yard goats grazed. The roof was held together by nails. Scattered on the ground were caps and bottles. I proposed a visit to Franco to try to restore the dwelling. I visited with him on October 11, 1970. Franco's health was still fairly good. He gave us the green light and today all can visit the house-museum which was opened on August 19, 1972.

20. Pardo Bazán, even before she was well known as a writer herself, significantly rebuffed Castro's attempt at friendship and literary collaboration. In 1880 Pardo Bazán had begun contributing articles and poetry to the most respected Galician periodical of the time, *La Ilustración Gallega y Asturiana* (*The Galician and Asturian Enlightenment*), directed by Murguía. Castro wrote a poem in Galician published on May 25, 1880, in Pardo Bazán's recently established magazine *La Revista de Galicia* (*The Galician Review*), acclaiming the latter's artistic abilities. The poem, entitled "En el abanico de Emilia Pardo Bazán" (On the Fan of Emilia Pardo Bazán), was the following:

Mimada polas Musas,
servida polas Gracias
cun corazón que vive de armonías,
nobre cantora das gallegas praias,
ben merecés reinar como reinades,
manífica, absoluta, soberana. (*Poemas sueltos* 579)

A favorite of the Muses,
served by the Graces
with a heart that lives of harmonies,
noble singer of the Galician beaches,
you deserve to reign as you reign,
magnificent, absolute, sovereign.

Castro did not even receive a copy of the magazine containing the poem. Pardo Bazán used Castro's laudatory poem to substantiate her own literary credibility but published nothing else of Castro's (Davies, 1984:

612–613). In a *Sar* poem (536–537) Castro surreptitiously criticizes Pardo Bazán, portraying her as contemptuous and immodest (March 109).

21. Juan Ramón Jiménez proposed, in a lecture on *modernismo* (*modernism*) delivered on February 17, 1953, "an outline for the history of nineteenth-century modern poetry which began with Curros Enríques, Vicente Medina, and Rosalía, and ended with Silva and Darío, all poets (often from the provinces or colonies) who rejected the stranglehold of official culture and conventional literary expression" (Davies, 1984: 616). Silva and Castro are often classified as premodernists. Camacho Guizado makes an interesting point, however, when he writes of Silva,

> ¡Menudo disgusto se iba a llevar el pobre José Asunción si, después de haber escrito la certera sátira "Sinfonía color de fresa con leche" contra los "colibríes decadentes rubendariacos," levantara la cabeza y viera que es considerado por muchos desaprensivamente como "precursor" de estos! (1990b: 411–412)
>
> *What a disappointment poor José Asunción would have if, after having written the appropriate satire "Symphony of the Color of Strawberries and Milk" against the "decadent poetry of Ruben Darío," were to resurrect and find himself unscrupulously labeled by many as the precursor [of that style]!*

When considering Silva and Castro within the context of modernism and poetry, it is important to remember that, for both authors, poetic form and style derive from content and not the other way around. Unlike Darío, they never filled their poetry with the purely decorative.

22. Silva, like Castro, suffered harsh critical review. According to Fogelquist he scandalized readers "porque en su poesía no respetó los convencionalismos literarios que ellos tenían por sagrados" (285, because in his poetry he did not respect the literary conventions that they held sacred). Clearly, contemporaries perceived Silva as dangerous to the literary and cultural status quo. In fact *De sobremesa* was published thirty years after Silva's death precisely because of its modern sexual and moral content (Mejía 474) and therefore was never evaluated during the corresponding modernist period. In the first edition of Silva's *Poesías* (*Poems*), editors also took it upon themselves to "correct" his poetry or to eliminate completely poems containing explicit sexual imagery, such as "Madrigal" and "Enfermedades de la niñez" (Mejía 473, Childhood Illnesses). Editors would modify successive editions as well.

Silva's insignificance at the time of his death is evident in the following newspaper commentary: "Anoche, en su cama, puso fin a sus días el joven José Asunción Silva. Parece que hacía versos" (García-Prada xxiv, Last night, in his bed, the young José Asunción Silva ended his life. It seems he wrote poetry). After Silva's death, critics persisted in biographical interpretations to denigrate further his person and oeuvre (Mejía 475). However, a small group of intellectuals liberal enough to admire Silva's original and emotional lyricism appreciated his work (Smith 61). Using his own considerable literary reputation, Unamuno helped to promote Silva's in his 1908 prologue to the first edition of Silva's *Poesías*. Unamuno writes prophetically that "Silva será un día orgullo de esta nuestra casta hispánica, que le produjo allá, en el sosiego primaveral de la jugosa Colombia, en el remanso Bogotá" (1965: xvi, Silva will one day become a pride for our hispanic race, which created him over there, in the spring tranquillity of fertile Colombia, in the pool of Bogotá).

Chapter III

1. Mayoral affirms that Castro's occasionally happy or candid depictions of love in *Cantares gallegos* "refleja una concepción del amor que no es la de Rosalía, sino la del pueblo gallego" (*R. de Castro* 81, reflects a conception of love which is not Rosalía's, but rather that of the Galician people). Yet even in *Cantares gallegos* Castro foreshadows her insistently pessimistic portrayal of love in later works, as I have tried to show.

2. Orjuela perceives in *Intimidades* evidence of an unhappy love affair, perhaps a result of unrequited love for the mysterious Adriana, who appears often in the verses of this volume. Orjuela notes, however, that "en el poemario aparecen también los nombres de otras mujeres que pueden haber contribuido a aumentar el desequilibrio de la vida sentimental del poeta: Paquita Martín, Natalia Tanco Armero y María Valenzuela, aunque con ellas parece insinuarse sólo una relación de amistad" (1990: 426, in the book of poems appear also the names of other women who may have contributed to the imbalance of the love life of the poet: Paquita Martín, Natalia Tanco Armero y María Valenzuela, although it seems that only friendship is suggested). Orjuela even suggests that Silva's unhappy experience with love may have influenced his decision to leave Bogotá for Paris (1977: 16). Perhaps if not the actual reason for leaving Bogotá, Silva's trip may have been a fortuitous coincidence, providing him with a chance to forget the disillusionment of his first love. Serrano Camargo affirms, however, that Silva's love poetry is the product of his own imagination and of romantic influence, except that dedicated to

Adriana, "musa real de su primera experiencia sentimental" (99, true muse of his first love experience).

3. Some romantics advised adultery because it could serve as an escape from a loveless marriage (Singer, 2: 299).

4. The fact that Silva mentions his nickname "el Casto José" (Chaste José), in *De sobremesa*, written shortly before he killed himself, is evidence that such a name deeply hurt him. Osiek maintains that by endowing his protagonist with so much sexual prowess, "Silva is able to counteract in a once-removed way the reputation he himself (as well as Fernández) had gained as being the chaste, virginal young man, without experience in sexual encounters" (1978: 124).

5. It is interesting to note that in Castro's case there is an underlying purpose to her insistent condemnation of carnal love as empty and unsatisfactory. In the nineteenth century women were unable openly to acknowledge their sexuality. Castro's female characters (unlike male characters like Flavio) generally show guilt whenever they engage in passionate love. As Susan Kirkpatrick notes, "nineteenth-century Spanish culture regarded any form of desire as incompatible with true femininity, and this prohibition dogged women writers' efforts to incorporate romantic subjectivity in images of the female self" (Feal 23). Mayoral avers in a general comment of Castro's works that "nos sorprende la falta de sensualidad, la ausencia de un canto al amor total, pleno, de carne y espíritu" (1974: 109, the lack of sensuality is surprising, the absence of singing to the total and complete love, of the flesh and of the spirit). Castro certainly could never have treated sensual love with complete freedom and have expected her work's publication. Yet she uses her disapproval of women's passionate side precisely to sidestep patriarchal society and to acknowledge the "fuego de ocultas pasiones" (*Orillas* 510, fire of hidden passions) that resides within the pallid women of her time. She wants to ground her poems and novels in human experience. As Poullain notes, "La revelación del amor carnal es presentada como un momento difícil y vergonzoso, que provoca hondo sufrimiento" (1974: 130, The revelation of carnal love is presented as a difficult and shameful moment, which causes deep suffering). Frequently Castro depicts and reproaches women who seek physical love, recognizing thereby that women possess sexual impulses and a passionate nature. In a covert manner, thus, she is acknowledging women as sexual beings with needs and desires in a historical period when society would have censored harshly such an admission on the part of a female writer. Indeed, in her novel *La hija del mar* Candora's illegitimate daughter, the symbol of her sexual transgression, kills herself (216).

Silva's portrayals of physical love typically go into more detail than do Castro's. But like Castro he condemns a repressive society in which women cannot express and explore their sexuality without guilt. In one poem a woman dreams of a sexual encounter with a man after praying to a crucifix. On waking, she experiences deep shame: "Al pie del Cristo contrita/Se traza en la blanca frente/Cruces con agua bendita" (*Intimidades* 215, Repentant at the foot of Christ/On her white brow she makes/The sign of the cross with holy water). In another poem Silva's speaker tells a young virgin to whisper quietly in his ear if she has dreamed, as he imagines, of her beloved's lips on her mouth and body (*Poesías varias* 110). By making love absurd, Silva points out its inability to give true meaning to an individual's life.

6. Both authors deplore the utter lack of humanitarian love in the world.

7. Cano Gaviria rejects the idea, one that Orjuela convincingly establishes (1976: 59–68), that María Bashkirtseff provides the model for Silva's Helena in *De sobremesa*. Cano Gaviria proposes that Carlos Holguín and one of his daughters are the principal models for Robert de Scilly Dancourt and Helena (613). Silva's arrival in Paris in October 1884 coincided with the publicity following the untimely death of María Bashkirtseff from tuberculosis. As an artist Bashkirtseff was much admired by her contemporaries. Her fame increased with the publication of her diary, which clearly influenced the form and theme of *De sobremesa* (Orjuela, 1990: 429). In fact, in his novel Silva expresses the impact Bashkirtseff's diary made on him: "Hay frases del Diario de la rusa que traducen tan sinceramente mis emociones, mis ambiciones y mis sueños, mi vida entera, que no habría podido jamás encontrar yo fórmulas más netas para anotar mis impresiones" (247, There are sentences in the Diary of the Russian woman that express so sincerely my emotions, my ambitions, and my dreams, my whole life, that I myself could never have found more precise words to jot down my impressions). Silva became obsessed with the tragic life and death of the Russian artist, but Orjuela indicates that her diary, not published in its entirety, created a false impression of María Bashkirtseff affirming that "la imagen idealizada de la joven no corresponde en realidad a la verdadera María, mujer vana, egoísta y ambiciosa" (1990: 429, the idolized image of the young woman does not correspond to the real María, a vain, selfish and ambitious woman).

8. In this poem, quite rare for his time, Silva does not condemn the young woman for producing an illegitimate child but instead censures the man for his actions: "Algo terrible sentirá tu alma/Infame libertino" (*Intimidades* 164, Your soul must feel some terrible emotion/Vile rake).

9. Through a Freudian interpretation, Mayoral relates Esperanza's

relationship with Ansot and her fear of birds to unresolved emotional conflicts between Castro and her own father (1974: 130). I would like to offer an additional analysis of Esperanza's abnormal and thematically significant fear of birds. Esperanza suffers from dementia as a result of her beloved Fausto's untimely death. In one scene she implores Alberto and the doctor who treats her to kill a bird she feels has penetrated her heart (168). In an elaborate pantomime, Ansot plucks out the imaginary bird to appease her. Castro may represent Fausto's pure soul symbolically and ironically through the birds that torment Esperanza (167–169, 182–183). Souls of the dead, in the Celtic tradition, become birds (Dutton 44). Galicians inherited a rich legacy of Celtic myths (Kulp-Hill 24). The pain Esperanza wishes to extirpate, represented through the hurtful birds, is the distressing reminder of Fausto's innocent love, forever lost and replaced by Ansot's depravity.

Chapter IV

1. To lessen the impression of Castro's unorthodoxy and thereby to improve her acceptance by critics, Murguía strategically inserted two poems containing religious references in the second edition of *Sar* (1909), which still open and close the volume today. These poems did not appear in the first edition, which was the only one Castro herself authorized (Mayoral, 1974: 35–36). Alonso Montero affirms that

> Murguía estaba empeñado en ofrecer una imagen religiosa de Rosalía que borrase otras imágenes más inquietantes, menos tradicionales....
> En la primera edición del libro el verso 80 de "Santa Escolástica" dice:
>
> *¿Por qué, aunque haya Dios, vence el infierno?*
>
> En la segunda edición la redacción es ésta:
>
> *¿Por qué, ya que hay Dios, vence el infierno?* (1972: 105–106)
>
> *Murguía stubbornly tried to convey a religious image of Rosalía to erase other more disquieting, less traditional images....*
> *In the first edition of the book verse 80 of "Saint Escolastica" says:*
>
> *Why, if there is a God, does hell triumph?*
>
> *In the second edition the wording is:*
>
> *Why, since there is a God, does hell triumph?*

Murguía's intentions were clearly to improve Castro's image in the eyes of conservatives of the day.

2. The image of the blindfold in Castro's poem recalls *La venda* (297–324, *The Blindfold*), an early play by Unamuno, an author whose religious crisis also resulted from attempts to understand God rationally.

3. In Silva's rejection of a merciful God there is perhaps also an indictment against his own tragic circumstances, which must have seemed unjust to him.

4. Silva was always aware of human mortality in contrast to nature. A telling incident reveals this acute sensitivity and his inherent pessimism. On November 26, 1865, the day Silva was born, his father planted some eucalyptus trees in the patio of their home. Ricardo Silva was fulfilling the proverb that a man should write a book, have a child, and plant a tree to live a meaningful life. According to Miramón, however, "Al mismo José Asunción, ya mayor, la existencia de esos árboles sembrados el día de su nacimiento llegó a preocuparle. "Tienen mi edad"—solía decir señalándolos a una persona amiga y por mucho tiempo vecina de su casa—"tienen mi edad y han de vivir mucho más que yo" (3, To José Asunción, as an adult, the existence of those trees planted on the day of his birth became worrisome. "They are my age"—he was want to say pointing them out to a friend who for many years was his neighbor—"they are my age and they will live much longer than I").

5. Refer to Bécquer's Rima LIII, "Volverán las oscuras golondrinas" (436, The Dark Swallows Will Return).

6. Death was a constant presence in Castro's and Silva's own lives, confirming their identification of existence with suffering. Not only did Castro correctly intuit her insidious cancer, but she also painfully witnessed the deaths of loved ones. In 1862 her beloved mother passed away. Castro dedicated an elegiac collection of poems to her, published by J. Compañel in Vigo (1863). Her son Adriano Honorato Alejandro died tragically in 1876, and in 1877 a daughter, Valentina, was stillborn (Mayoral, 1, 1993: xxii-xxiii).

Silva also suffered considerable personal loss in his brief life. He was the oldest of six children, three of whom died in infancy or early childhood (Charry Lara, 1989: 1). In 1889 his father, Ricardo, passed away, and in 1891 his sister Elvira died unexpectedly. Two of Silva's relatives had committed suicide, which most likely clouded his worldview further. In 1860 his second cousin Guillermo Silva, son of Antonio María, shot himself because his father would not allow him to leave Hatogrande to celebrate Christmas Eve in Bogotá. Another cousin, Enrique Villar, also shot himself in Mexico (Osiek, 1978: 18; Socarrás 17–18).

7. This poem refers to the death of Castro's son Adriano Honorato Alejandro in 1876 before his second birthday as a result of a fall from a table. His tragic death tormented Castro all her life (Mayoral, 1976: 75).

8. Elvira's death was a particularly cruel blow for Silva. She was not only a beloved sister but a trusted confidant. Her death could not have come at a worse time for him as he was struggling with bankruptcy proceedings stemming from the financial crisis his father had left him at his death.

On the night of January 5, 1891, Elvira stepped out on the balcony to see a comet (Osiek, 1978: 36). She took ill suddenly as a result of the cold air. But her death may best be attributed to misdiagnosis. Wrongly, her doctor treated her for typhoid and recommended the customary fasting regimen. Gómez, a professor of medicine, amended his colleague's diagnosis and began immediate treatment for pneumonia (Mutis Durán 800–801); but it was too late. Her uncommon beauty and tragic death at twenty-one inspired numerous literary tributes, including a poem by Jorge Isaacs. In a letter thanking friend Eduardo Villa Ricaurte for his poem dedicated to Elvira, Silva passionately wrote, "Yo sé para el resto de lo que viva que lo más querido, lo más encantador que exista, puede desaparecer en unos segundos, y para siempre temeré la llegada repentina de la Muerte" (*Correspondencia* 676, I am aware that for the rest of my life the most beloved, the most lovely [person], may disappear in a few seconds, and forever more I shall fear the sudden arrival of Death).

9. At times Castro's physical pain from her cancer was so acute that when she spoke of death she hoped fervently that hers would be as rapid as her mother's had been. But in a letter to her husband detailing a recent illness, she correctly anticipates that she will die slowly (*Cartas* 603–604, *Letters*). Murguía confirms that "para morir tuvo que sufrir una agonía de tres días" (Kulp 7–8, to die she suffered agony for three days). Mayoral feelingly writes "Consuela pensar que aquel julio de 1885 fue lluvioso y gris. Lo cuenta el poeta Lisardo Barreira que fue a verla poco antes de morir: 'Llovía y el sol alumbraba apenas entre las nubes'. Al menos en aquella ocasión la naturaleza ya que no la muerte fue piadosa con Rosalía" (*Actas* 351, It is consoling to think that that July of 1885 was rainy and gray. The poet Lisardo Barreira who went to see her shortly before her death tells us this: 'It was raining and the sun barely shone through the clouds.' At least on that occasion nature if not death took pity on Rosalía).

10. Murguía writes that shortly before his wife died, "marchó a Carril con los suyos. Quería ver el mar antes de morir: el mar, que había sido siempre, en la Naturaleza, su amor predilecto. Pero en aquellas orillas que

le recordaban otras horas felices, se sintió ya tan rendida, que apenas podía dejar su aposento" (1993: 455, she went to Carril with her family. She wanted to behold the sea before dying: the sea, which of nature had always been her favorite. But on those shores which brought back other happy moments, she felt so exhausted, that she was hardly able to leave her room). Castro addressed her last wish before she died at noon on July 15, 1885, to her oldest daughter Alejandra: "Abride a ventana que quero ver o mar" (García Sabell 50, Open the window for I wish to watch the sea). The sea was not visible from La Matanza, her home in Padrón, and her request has been attributed to her delirium. Yet she so often associated the sea with death in her works, that these final words seem to echo symbolically her yearning for surcease from so much suffering.

11. Silva left no note explaining his suicide. A large quantity of Turkish cigarette butts were in the ashtray of his bedroom, showing how long he agonized about his decision during the early morning hours of that rainy Sunday, May 24, 1896 (Cuervo Márquez 510). The day before Silva killed himself, he visited the office of his friend Dr. Juan Evangelista Manrique on some pretext. During the examination Silva lightly inquired as to the location of the human heart. Manrique demonstrated the precise position by drawing a cross for him with a pencil (Cuervo Márquez 40–41). Perhaps Silva's visit to Manrique was an unconscious cry for help. It was not a lack of religious beliefs, however, that caused Silva to take his own life as many critics maintain (Litvak 379). It was something much less complicated and, for that reason, much more tragic. Silva chose death because he was financially ruined. After the failure of his polychromatic cement tile business, surrounded by creditors, Silva uttered these ominous words, "A mí me verán primero muerto que pálido" (Miramón 155, They will see me first dead than pale [shamed]). Heroic efforts to succeed financially reveal his desire to live—but to live with his pride intact. Like his father's, Silva's business acumen was very weak. Tragically—as it turned out—Silva had to end his formal schooling at age sixteen to help his father in his import store (Osiek, 1978: 27). In 1884 his great-uncle Antonio María offered to fulfill Silva's cherished dream of living with him in Paris and provide him with a formal education in Europe. As he was crossing the Atlantic, however, Antonio María died, and Silva did not receive the education he had hoped for (Osiek, 1978: 27–28). This unlucky circumstance proved fatal. If Silva had been able to pursue a career such as medicine, which interested him, he would not have had to depend on commercial skills for survival.

In the overall comparison of Silva and Castro, it becomes evident that whereas Silva dwells on the theme of suicide as a response to personal suffering and disillusionment, Castro at times counterbalances suicidal impulses by looking outward to the world, to nature and society, as she sublimates her own grief in an identification with the suffering of all humanity.

12. To commit suicide, Silva himself used a rusty Smith and Wesson revolver that had once belonged to his father (Cuervo Márquez 510). Sanín Cano comments that on leaving the protective environment of childhood, Silva was unequipped emotionally and temperamentally to cope with the hardships of life (1985: 244).

13. One afternoon in 1896, as Silva and close friend Baldomero Sanín Cano were crossing a street, a woman killed herself before their eyes by jumping from a high balcony. Sanín Cano was so affected by what he had witnessed that he thought he would be ill but Silva was unperturbed. He first informed Sanín Cano that the woman had a perfect right to kill herself and, because she was mentally unbalanced, was useless and dangerous (Osiek, 1978: 45–48). Miramón affirms

> El pensamiento de la muerte por voluntad y consumación propia pareció siempre a la inteligencia y al sentimiento de José Asunción Silva una cosa natural y lógica. Frecuentemente abordaba el tema del suicidio y el de la muerte. De los suicidas decía, citando a Barrés, que se matan por falta de imaginación. Y sobre el libre albedrío que determina estos desenlaces usaba esta comparación: "El hombre muere de suicidio como suele morir de tifus. Ambas son enfermedades infecciosas. La estadística no deja duda sobre la semejanza de ellas. Las cifras de la una y de la otra se prolongan en direcciones paralelas. ¿Por qué no habrán hecho un cementerio aparte para los que mueren de tifus?" (159)
>
> *The thought of death by one's own will and suicide seemed a natural and logical thing to José Asunción Silva's intelligence and feelings. He frequently treated the themes of suicide and death. About people who committed suicide he said, citing Barrés, that they kill themselves because they lack imagination. And about the free will that determines these endings he used this comparison: "Man dies from suicide as from typhoid. Both are infectious diseases. Statistics leave no doubt as to their likeness. The numbers of one and the other parallel each other. Why haven't they laid out a separate cemetery for those that die from typhoid?"*

14. Castro's and Silva's own remains were exhumed and transferred in public recognition of their accomplishments years after their deaths.

Castro was originally buried in the small cemetery of Adina beside her mother as she had wished. On May 25, 1891, she was removed to the Pantheon of Illustrious Galicians at the Church of the Visitation in the Convent of Santo Domingo de Bonaval in Santiago (García Martí 122–123). As testimony to Castro's mythification in Galicia following her death, the notary, Jesús Fernández Suárez, states that upon transferring her remains to the cemetery in Santiago six years after her passing, her body and clothing emerged completely intact and the bouquet of pansies eldest daughter Alejandra had placed in her mother's tomb, "ligeramente decolorados y cual si estuviesen recientemente cortados" (Costa Clavell 95, slightly discolored as if they had been cut recently).

In Silva's case, as civil law was subject to church law, he was originally buried in the suicide cemetery not far from the city dump. Approximately thirty-eight years later he was removed to the family pantheon and buried beside his sister Elvira (Osiek, 1978: 48).

Bibliography

Albert Robatto, Matilde. *Rosalía de Castro y Emilia Pardo Bazán: Afinidades y contrastes*. A Coruña: Ediciós de Castro, 1995.

_____. *Rosalía de Castro y la condición femenina*. Madrid: Partenón, 1981.

Aldaz, Anna-Marie, and Barbara N. Gantt. Introduction to *Poems, Rosalía de Castro*. New York: State U of New York P, 1991. 1–16.

Alonso Montero, Xesús. "Prólogo." *En las orillas del Sar*. Salamanca: Anaya, 1964. 5–23.

Alonso Montero, Xesús. *Rosalía de Castro*. Madrid: Júcar, 1972.

Alvarez Sanagustín, Alberto. "Un personaje extraño de Rosalía: el duque de la gloria." *Actas do congreso internacional de estudios sobre Rosalía de e o seu tempo*. Vol. 1. Santiago de Compostela: Universidad de Santiago de Compostela, 1986. 503–510.

Arguedas, Alcides. "La Danza de las sombras." *Obras completas*. Mexico: Impresiones Modernas, 1959. 855–866.

Balbontín, José Antonio. "Rosalía de Castro." *Three Spanish Poets*. London: Redman, 1961. 15–55.

Barco, Pablo del. "Caminando con las botas azules." *CHA* 424–426 (1985): 57–61.

Bar-Lewaw, Itzhak. "José Asunción Silva, apuntes para su obra." *Temas literarios iberoamericanos*. Mexico: Costa-Amic, 1961. 49–77.

Basdekis, Demetrios. "Unamuno y Rosalía." *Revista Grial* 11 (1965): 83–85.

Bécquer, Gustavo Adolfo. *Obras completas*. 13th ed. Madrid: Aguilar, 1969.

Blanco Fombona, Rufino. "José Asunción Silva." *Poesía y prosa de José Asunción Silva*. Bogotá: Biblioteca Básica Colombiano, 1979. 444–469.

Bouza Brey, Fermín. "La joven Rosalía en Compostela (1852–1856)." *CEG* 10 (1955): 201–257.

Bowra, C. M. "El experimento creativo: José Asunción Silva." *José Asunción Silva, vida y creación*. Bogotá: Procultura, 1985. 75–78.

Brigard Silva, Camilo de. "El infortunio comercial de Silva." *Obras completas de José Asunción Silva.* Bogotá: Banco de la República, 1965. 388–413.

_____. "Silva en Caracas." *Poesía y prosa de José Asunción Silva.* Bogotá: Biblioteca Básica Colombiana, 1979. 717–729.

Camacho Guizado, Eduardo. *La poesía de José Asunción Silva.* Bogotá: Universidad de los Andes, 1968.

_____. "Poética y poesía de Silva." *José Asunción Silva, obra completa.* Nanterre: Université Paris X, 1990a. 533–566.

_____. "Prólogo." *José Asunción Silva, obra completa.* Venezuela: Biblioteca Ayacucho, 1977. ix–lii.

_____. "Silva ante el modernismo." *José Asunción Silva, obra completa.* Nanterre: Université Paris X, 1990b. 411–421.

Cano Gaviria, Ricardo. "Mímesis y 'pacto biográfico' en algunas prosas de Silva y en *De sobremesa.*" *José Asunción Silva, obra completa.* Nanterre: Université Paris X, 1990. 596–622.

Carballo Calero, Ricardo. "Referencias a Rosalía en cartas de sus contemporáneos." *CEG* 54 (1958): 303–313.

Carrier, Warren. "Baudelaire y Silva." *RI* 7 (1943–44): 39–48.

Castagnino, Raul H. "Correspondencia privada y comercial de José Asunción Silva." *Escritores hispanoamericanos desde otros ángulos de simpatía.* Buenos Aires: Nova, 1971. 163–172.

Castillo, Homero. "Función del tiempo en 'Los maderos de San Juan.'" *Hispania* 47 (1964): 703–704.

Castro, Rosalía de. *Obras completas.* 2 vols. Madrid: Biblioteca Castro, 1993.

Cernuda, Luis. "Rosalía de Castro." *Estudios sobre poesía española contemporánea.* Madrid: Guadarrama, 1957. 59–69.

Charry Lara, Fernando. *José Asunción Silva.* Bogotá: Procultura, 1989.

_____, ed. *José Asunción Silva, vida y creación.* Bogotá: Procultura, 1985.

Ciplijauskaite, Birute. "La 'cárcel estrecha' y sus modulaciones." *Actas do congreso internacional de estudios sobre Rosalía de Castro e o seu tempo.* Vol. 2. Santiago de Compostela: Universidad de Santiago de Compostela, 1986. 321–329.

Cirlot, J. E. *A Dictionary of Symbols.* New York: Philosophical Library, 1962.

Clemessy, Nelly. "Unas claves posibles de la sensibilidad romántica de Rosalía de Castro en El primer loco." *Actas do congreso internacional de estudios sobre Rosalía de Castro e o seu tempo.* Vol. 1. Santiago de Compostela: Universidad de Santiago de Compostela, 1986. 523–527.

Consello-da-Cultura-Galega; Universidad de Santiago de Compostela. *Actas do congreso internacional de estudios sobre Rosalía de Castro e o seu tempo*. 3 vols. Santiago de Compostela: Universidad de Santiago de Compostela, 1986.

Corona Marzol, Gonzalo. "Una lectura de Rosalía." *RL* 44 (1982): 25–62.

Costa Clavell, Javier. *Rosalía de Castro*. Barcelona: Plaza y Janes, 1967.

Courteau, Joannna. "Language and Ethnicity: The Case of Rosalía de Castro." *Language and Ethnicity, Focusschrift in Honor of Joshua A. Fishman on the Occasion of his 65th Birthday*. Amsterdam/Philadelphia: Benjamins, 1991. 83–94.

_____. *The Poetics of Rosalía de Castro's Negra Sombra*. New York: Mellen P, 1995.

Cross, Leland W. "Poe y Silva: Unas palabras de disensión." *Hispania* 44 (1961): 647–651.

Cuervo Márquez, Emilio. "José Asunción Silva, su vida y su obra." *Poesía y Prosa José A. Silva*. Bogotá: Biblioteca Básica Colombiana, 1979. 487–512.

Davies, Catherine. "Rosalía's 'camino blanco': The Way of Goodness." *Readings in Spanish and Portuguese Poetry for Geoffrey Connell*. Glasgow: U of Glasgow P, 1985. 16–27.

_____. "Rosalía de Castro, criticism 1950–1989: The Need for a New Approach." *BHS* 60 (1983): 211–219.

_____. "Rosalía de Castro's Later Poetry and Anti-Regionalism in Spain." *MLR* 79 (1984): 609–619.

Díaz, Nidia. *La protesta social en la obra de Rosalía de Castro*. Vigo: Galaxia, 1976.

Dutton, Brian, ed. *Gonzalo de Berceo, los milagros de nuestra señora*. London: Tamesis, 1971.

Feal, Carlos. "El oscuro sujeto del deseo romántico: De Espronceda a Rosalía." *RHM* 47 (1944): 15–28.

Filgueira Valverde, José. "Cinco visiones contemporáneas sobre Rosalía de Castro." *Rosalía de Castro, la luz de la negra sombra*. Madrid: Silex, 1985. 189–190.

Fogelquist, Donald F. "José Asunción Silva y Heinrich Heine." *RHM* 20 (1954): 282–294.

Galanes Lewis, Adriana. "La hija del mar (1859): Llave a los conflictivos espacios interiores en la expresión literaria de Rosalía de Castro." *Hispano* 32–33 (1988–90): 17–31.

García Martí, Victoriano. "Rosalía de Castro o el dolor de vivir." *Rosalía de Castro, obras completas*. Madrid: Aguilar, 1972. 9–203.

García-Prada, Carlos. "Introducción." *José Asunción Silva, prosas y versos.* Madrid: Iberoamericanas, 1942. ix–xxxv.

García Sabell, Domingo. "Rosalía y su sombra." *7 (Siete) ensayos sobre Rosalía.* Vigo: Galaxia, 1952. 41–56.

Gicovate, Bernardo. "El modernismo y José Asunción Silva." *José Asunción Silva, obra completa.* Nanterre: Université Paris X, 1990. 393–410.

_____. "Estructura y significado en la poesía de José Asunción Silva." *RI* 24 (1959): 327–331.

_____. "José Asunción Silva y la decadencia europea." *José Asunción Silva, vida y creación.* Bogotá: Procultura, 1985. 107–123.

Hamilton, Carlos D. *Nuevo lenguaje poético de Silva a Neruda.* Bogotá: Caro y Cuervo, 1965.

Henríquez Ureña, Max. "José Asunción Silva." *Breve historia del modernismo.* Mexico: Fondo de Cultura Económica, 1962. 133–155.

Holguín, Andrés. "El sentido del misterio en Silva." *José Asunción Silva, vida y creación.* Bogotá: Procultura, 1985. 263–274.

Jiménez, Juan Ramón. "José Asunción Silva." *Españoles de tres mundos.* Madrid: Aguado, 1960. 136–139.

_____. "Rosalía de Castro." *Españoles de tres mundos.* Madrid: Aguado, 1960. 106–108.

Kulp, Kathleen. *Manner and Mood in Rosalía de Castro.* Madrid: Porrua Turanzas, 1968.

Kulp-Hill, Kathleen. *Rosalía de Castro.* Boston: Twayne, 1977.

Laín Entralgo, Pedro. *Antropología médica para clínicos.* Barcelona: Salvat, 1986.

_____. "Hoy y mañana." *Teatro del mundo.* Madrid: Espasa-Calpe, 1986. 323–347.

Lapesa, Rafael. "Tres poetas ante la soledad: Bécquer, Rosalía y Machado." *De Ayala a Ayala, estudios literarios y estilísticos.* Madrid: Istmo, 1988. 243–272.

Lázaro, Angel. *Rosalía de Castro.* Madrid: Compañía Bibliográfica Española, 1966.

Litvak, Lily. "José Asunción Silva." *Latin American Writers.* Vol. 1. New York: Scribner's, 1989. 377–384.

Loveluck, Juan. "De sobremesa, novela desconocida del modernismo." *RI* 31 (1965): 17–32.

McClelland, I. L. "Bécquer, Rubén Darío, and Rosalía de Castro." *Liverpool Studies in Spanish Literature.* Liverpool: Inst. of Hispanic Studies, 1940. 240–264.

McGrady, Donald. "Una caricatura literaria de José Asunción Silva."

Poesía y prosa de José Asunción Silva. Bogotá: Biblioteca Básica Colombiana, 1979. 680–689.

Machado da Rosa, Alberto. "Heine in Spain (1856–67)—Relations with Rosalía de Castro." *Monatshefte* 49 (1957): 65–82.

Madariaga, Salvador de. "Rosalía de Castro." *Mujeres españolas*. Madrid: Espasa-Calpe, 1975. 271–321.

Manrique, Juan Evangelista. "José Asunción Silva (Recuerdos íntimos)." *José Asunción Silva, vida y creación*. Bogotá: Procultura, 1985. 35–41.

March, Kathleen, N. "Rosalía de Castro." *Spanish Women Writers: A Bio-Bibliographical Source Book*. Westport, CT: Greenwood P, 1993. 104–112.

Martín, Elvira. "Rosalía de Castro." *Tres mujeres gallegas del siglo XIX*. Barcelona: Aedos, 1962. 87–154.

Martinengo, Alessandro. "Papeles inéditos de Miguel de Unamuno referentes a la edición de las poesías de Silva." *Thesaurus* 16 (1961): 740–745.

Martínez Ruiz, José. "Rosalía de Castro." *Clásicos y modernos*. Buenos Aires: Losada, 1939. 37–41.

Martínez Torner, Eduardo. *Lírica hispánica, relaciones entre lo popular y lo culto*. Madrid: Castalia, 1966.

Maya, Rafael. "José Asunción Silva, el poeta y el prosista." *José Asunción Silva, vida y creación*. Bogotá: Procultura, 1985. 89–106.

Mayoral, Marina, ed. *Escritoras románticas españolas*. Madrid: Fundación Banco Exterior, 1990.

_____. "Introducción." *Obras completas, Rosalía de Castro*. Vol. 1. Madrid: Biblioteca, Castro, 1993. xii–xxiii.

_____. "Introducción." *Obras completas, Rosalía de Castro*. Vol. 2. Madrid: Biblioteca, Castro, 1993. xii–xxvi.

_____. "Introducción y notas." *En las orillas del Sar*. Madrid: Castalia, 1976. 9–46.

_____. "La hija del mar: Biografía, confesión lírica y folletín." *La narrativa romántica*. Genoa: Biblioteca di Lett, 1988. 80–88.

_____. *La poesía de Rosalía de Castro*. Madrid: Gredos, 1974.

_____. *Rosalía de Castro*. Madrid: Cátedra, 1986.

_____. "La voz del narrador desde *La hija del mar* a *El primer loco*: Un largo camino hacia la objetividad narrativa." *Actas do congreso internacional de estudios sobre Rosalía de Castro e o seu tempo*. Vol. 1. Santiago de Compostela: Universidad de Santiago de Compostela, 1986. 341–366.

Mejía, Gustavo. "José Asunción Silva: sus textos, su crítica." *José Asunción Silva, obra completa*. Nanterre: Université Paris X, 1990. 471–499.

Miller La Follette, Martha. "Parallels in Rosalía de Castro and Emily Dickinson." *Comparatist* 5 (1981): 3–9.

_____. "Rosalía de Castro and Her Context." *Ensayos de literatura europea e hispanoamericana*. San Sebastián: Universidad del País Vasco, 1990. 325–328.

Miramón, Alberto. *José Asunción Silva*. Colombia: Nacional, 1937.

Montero, Eugenio. *Rosalía de Castro, la luz de la negra sombra*. Madrid: Silex, 1985.

Murguía, Manuel. "Prólogo." *En las orillas del Sar*. Madrid: Biblioteca Castro, 1993. 445–456.

_____. "Rosalía de Castro." *Los precursores*. Buenos Aires: Emecé, 1944. 132–155.

Mutis Durán, Santiago, and J. G. Cobo Borda, eds. *Poesía y prosa José Asunción Silva*. Bogotá: Biblioteca Básica Colombiana, 1979.

Nogales de Muniz, María Antonia. *Irradiación de Rosalía de Castro*. Barcelona: Estrada, 1966.

Orjuela, Héctor H. *"De sobremesa" y otros estudios sobre José Asunción Silva*. Bogotá: Caro y Cuervo, 1976.

_____. "Estudio preliminar." *José Asunción Silva, "Intimidades."* Bogotá: Caro y Cuervo, 1977. 1–42.

_____, ed. *José Asunción Silva, obra completa*. Nanterre: Université Paris X, 1990.

Ortega y Gasset, José. *Historia como sistema*. 1935 ed. Vol. 6. Madrid: Revista de Occidente, 1947.

_____. *Meditación de la técnica*. 4th ed. Madrid: Revista de Occidente, 1961.

Osiek, Betty Tyree. *José Asunción Silva*. Boston: Twayne, 1978.

_____. *José Asunción Silva, Estudio estilístico de su poesía*. Mexico: Edison, 1968.

Pardo Bazán, Emilia. "La poesía regional gallega." *Obras completas*. Vol. 3. Madrid: Aguilar, 1973. 671–688.

Pérez, Janet. "Rosalía de Castro." *Modern and Contemporary Spanish Women Poets*. New York: Twayne, 1996. 30–37.

Piñeiro, Ramón. "A Saudade en Rosalía." *7 (Siete) ensayos sobre Rosalía*. Vigo: Galaxia, 1952. 95–109.

Pociña, Andrés. "La crítica feminista ante la persona y la obra de Rosalía de Castro." *Crítica y ficción literaria: Mujeres españolas contemporáneas*. Granada: Universidad de Granada, 1989. 61–83.

Poe, Edgar Allan. *Complete Poems*. New York: Gramercy, 1992.

Poullain, Claude. *Rosalía de Castro de Murguía y su obra literaria*. Madrid: Nacional, 1974.

_____. "Valor y sentido de la novela de Rosalía Castro de Murguía, *El caballero de las botas azules*." *CEG* 25 (1956): 37–69.

Rof Carballo, J. "Rosalía, Anima galaica." *7 (Siete) ensayos sobre Rosalía.* Vigo: Galaxia, 1952. 111–149.

Sánchez Mora, Elena. "Rosalía de Castro: ¿Bachillera o ángel del hogar?" *Actas do congreso internacional de estudios sobre Rosalía de Castro e o seu tempo.* Vol. 1. Santiago de Compostela: Universidad de Santiago de Compostela, 1986. 251–257.

Sanín Cano, Baldomero. "Notas a la obra de Silva." *José Asunción Silva, vida y creación.* Bogotá: Procultura, 1985. 233–245.

_____. "Recuerdos de J. A. Silva." *Poesía y prosa José Asunción Silva.* Bogotá: Biblioteca Básica Colombiana, 1979. 513–517.

Schulman, Ivan A. "Tiempo e imagen en la poesía de José Asunción Silva." *Génesis del modernismo.* Mexico: Colegio de Mexico, 1966. 188–215.

Schwartz, Kessel. "Rosalía de Castro's *En las orillas del Sar*: A Psychoanalytic Interpretation." *Symposium* 26 (1972): 363–375.

Schwartz, Rosalinda J. "En busca de Silva." *José Asunción Silva, vida y creación.* Bogotá: Procultura, 1985. 371–384.

Serrano Camargo, Rafael. *Silva: imagen y estudio analítico del poeta.* Bogotá: Tercer Mundo, 1987.

Shaw, D. L. "Rosalía de Castro." *Historia de la literatura española, el siglo XIX.* Barcelona: Ariel, 1986. 168–177.

Silva, José Asunción. *Obra completa.* Nanterre: Université Paris X, 1990.

Singer, Irving. *The Nature of Love.* 3 vols. Chicago: U of Chicago P, 1984.

Sixto Seco, Agustín. "Cinco visiones contemporáneas sobre Rosalía de Castro." *Rosalía de Castro, la luz de la negra sombra.* Madrid: Silex, 1985. 192–193.

Smith, Mark I. "Arte y burguesía: Silva en el ambiente bogotano." *José Asunción Silva, vida y creación.* Bogotá: Procultura, 1985. 57–62.

Socarrás, José Francisco. "A manera de introducción, la personalidad de José Asunción Silva." *Silva, imagen y estudio analítico del poeta.* Bogotá: Tercer Mundo, 1987. 13–51.

Stevens, Shelley. *Rosalía de Castro and the Galician Revival.* London: Tamesis, 1996.

Tirrell, Sister Mary Pierre. *La mística de la saudade.* Madrid: Jura, 1951.

Torres Ríoseco, Arturo. "José Asunción Silva." *Precursores del modernismo.* New York: Las Américas, 1963. 95–122.

_____. "Las teorías poéticas de Poe y el caso Silva." *José Asunción Silva, vida y creación.* Bogotá: Procultura, 1985. 201–209.

Unamuno, Miguel de. "José Asunción Silva." *Poesía y prosa, José Asunción Silva.* Bogotá: Biblioteca Básica Colombiana, 1979. 419–424.

_____. "Prólogo." *Obras completas de José Asunción Silva.* Bogotá: Banco de la República, 1965. v–xvi.

Varela Jácome, Benito. "Emilia Pardo Bazán, Rosalía de Castro y Murguía." *CEG* 6 (1951): 405–429.
____. "Rosalía de Castro, novelista." *CEG* 14 (1958): 57–86.
Varela, José Luis. "Rosalía y la saudade." *Poesía y restauración cultural de Galicia en el siglo XIX*. Madrid: Gredos, 1958. 145–211.
Vázquez Rey, Antonio. *Esbozo para unha biografía de Rosalía.* A Coruña: Edición do Castro, 1995.
Zubiri, Xavier. *Sobre el hombre.* Madrid: Alianza, 1986.
____. *Estructura dinámica de la realidad.* Madrid: Alianza, 1995.

Index